What Would You Do If You Weren't Afraid?

As someone who worked with Michal I can honestly say that she lives and demonstrates the wisdom she writes about. If you want to learn how to combine a meaningful and spiritual life with a successful career – this is a must read.

Nicola Mendelsohn CBE,
Head of Global Business Group, Meta

Michal Oshman writes from the heart. She shares her personal life experiences candidly and openly to connect meaningfully with the reader. Her life lessons are sure to resonate with any reader curious about how to live a meaningful life in a very complex world. This book is equally relevant in the working and personal dimensions of our lives.

Loren I. Shuster, *Chief People Officer & Head of Corporate Affairs, The LEGO Group*

This special book by Michal Oshman will change how you approach your life, in a spiritual as well as practical way. The book is truly empowering and allows you to connect and learn from the author's personal life experiences in a meaningful way

Julien Wettstein, *Head of Editorial for Europe, Middle East and Africa, LinkedIn*

There are so many light-bulb moments. I couldn't wait to start this and, once I did, I couldn't put it down. Meaningful, useful, practical, and with so many aspects that I can use to support individuals to embed Equity, Diversity, and Inclusion into their daily work. This book touches the soul and provides many amazing life lessons. Thank you Michal Oshman for a beautiful and incredibly inspiring read. I'm looking forward to sharing all the learnings with my network.

Priscilla Balfour,
Global Head of Diversity and Inclusion, Unilever

Michal has a wonderful way of marrying old wisdom with new contexts. You'll be glad you took a leap of faith and explored this book, no matter what faith you hold or don't. It's a manual for life, for leadership, and for all of us.

Diana Barea,
Managing Director of Strategy, Accenture

This book is important reading for anyone who is touched in some way, by fear and anxiety. For most of us, fear and anxiety are all-too-familiar bedfellows. Whether, as Oshman puts it, we fear of "failing, messing up or ageing", fear touches us all. And it's against this backdrop, that Oshman offers refreshing and disarmingly honest words, drawing on the deep wells of Jewish thought and experience, to help readers reflect on how they might live a life full of meaning and purpose.

Kenny Temowo,
Executive Coach, Netflix

This book was extremely inspiring, helpful, and practical. It took the most difficult mystical concepts, explained them in a very clear way, and then gave practical ways to apply these concepts to improve life quality and deeper purpose at work, with family, and of course, improve our relationship with our spirtual reality.

Idit Gazit-Berger, *Head of Digital Native,*
Central Eastern Europe and MEA, Microsoft

For my Auntie Sara who teaches me
bravery, optimism and positivity

MICHAL OSHMAN

FORMERLY HEAD OF COMPANY CULTURE AT TIKTOK
AND INTERNATIONAL LEADERSHIP DEVELOPMENT
EXECUTIVE AT FACEBOOK

What Would You Do If You Weren't Afraid?

CREATING A MEANINGFUL LIFE IN UNCERTAIN TIMES

Contents

1
THE DISCOVERY

'The two most important days in your life are the day you are born and the day you find out why.'

Mark Twain

THE
DISCOVERY

"The two most important days in your life are the day you are born and the day you find out why."

—Mark Twain

On my first day at Facebook (now Meta), as I stood at the company reception desk about to embark on what was, at the time, the most meaningful job of my career, something caught my eye. It was a question on the wall and it asked:

What would you do if you weren't afraid?

This question hit me because, despite serving as a commanding officer in the Israeli army, holding several university degrees and working as a senior leader at top banks, advertising, PR and tech companies, all my life, in one way or another, I had been just that: afraid.

On the surface, my life at this point was a success story. I was born in Israel, in a secular Jewish household, the eldest daughter of two intelligent and accomplished parents. I was raised 'culturally Jewish', respectful of our heritage without much practice of our religion. After graduating high school I'd carried out compulsory military service where, within the first two weeks, I was selected to lead an entire unit. I'd married a caring, loving, smart man and we had three (now four) beautiful children. Since relocating to the UK, I'd had a successful career coaching and consulting with some of the best leadership talent I could ever imagine working with, at companies like Danone, WPP, eBay and, starting that day, Facebook. Yes, my life appeared to be an impressive series of achievements.

Now let me tell you the *real* story.

At that point in my life, and for as long as I could remember, I had been suffering from anxiety. The kind that permeates every aspect of your life and consumes every waking thought. This anxiety meant that my mind would naturally drift to the worst-case scenario in any situation. If my friend texted to let me know she was on her way to my house, I would imagine her having a car crash on the way. I would never suggest a time to meet up because then I would be complicit in her death. Each time one of my children asked me to sign a permission form for a school trip or a day at the museum, it felt like I was signing their death sentence.

As anyone suffering from anxiety can attest, these imaginary scenarios can have very real effects on the mind and body. Those intrusive thoughts would send waves of heat coursing through my entire body. I'd become short of breath – all because of fear: fear that my children would get lost, forgotten or kidnapped at the museum. That's how immediate negative outcomes were to me. They would flash into my head, then I would ruminate on them again and again, imagining them vividly, until in my mind (and body) they became reality.

Was there a reason for my anxiety? For the moments of despair that would wash over me? For my fears? Any psychologist would say there certainly was. When I was growing up, my father was Israel's top forensic pathologist. Throughout his career he performed tens of thousands of autopsies on children and adults who had died an unnatural death. He also conducted physical examinations of women and children who had been sexually assaulted or raped. He was called to visit crime scenes and sites of terror attacks on a daily basis. After conducting autopsies, he faced the hardest part of his job: meeting the parents, partners or children of the victims, and telling them what had happened to their loved ones. At home, I'd sometimes pass his desk and see the photographs spilling from his briefcase – horrific photographs that showed in graphic detail what humans are capable of doing to each other. Shows like *CSI: Crime Scene Investigation* never show you what the children of forensic pathologists are subject to. Of course, my father did what he could to shield me from these sights, but for my entire childhood I was surrounded by death and the horrors of humanity.

Death poked its nose in from other directions, too. My grandparents on both sides were Holocaust survivors and their first-hand experience of genocide left them permanently traumatised. Therefore, the murder of six million Jews by the Nazis in the Second World War was not a piece of history to me: it was an integral part of my life from the moment I was born. My grandmother's nightmares – I would hear her screaming that the Nazis were coming – were my nightly lullabies. She used to hoard food in preparation for another Holocaust. She would try to force me to eat chicken soup to ensure I didn't suffer the starvation she had experienced. To this day I still can't eat chicken soup. Even the smell of it makes me nauseous.

My grandparents' deeply traumatic Holocaust experiences left their imprint on both my parents, too. They were raised with a survival mindset and, as a result, so was I. Yes, I was born to a professor of medicine and a teacher, and therefore I had access to education and opportunities that not everyone has. Yet, in our home, there was no space for being carefree; the imperative was to ensure that there was food to eat, that we were safe from harm and that we made ourselves indispensable to the world. Everything else was a physical or emotional luxury. Is it any wonder I feared death? Death just seemed more *likely* than life. There were so many things that could go wrong, so many illnesses I could contract, so many accidents that could happen.

During my teenage years, Israel was subject to constant terror attacks. There were frequent bombings, often on public transport. Every bus journey began with me doing a quick scan of the other passengers, silently registering who was carrying a large backpack. My father would tell me to always sit by the window on the bus and open it to minimise injuries in case of an explosion. My greatest fear wasn't the explosion, getting injured or even dying, it was the fear of ending up as a corpse in my father's morgue. I would fear his reaction to his daughter's dead body, the pain and horror that would cause him.

And it wasn't just death I feared, but a whole host of other things: messing up, being rejected, ageing, not being taken seriously, disappointing people or failing. My father is extremely hard-working and was successful in both his career and in academia. My mother holds numerous degrees and is an accomplished teacher. They expected the same success from their eldest daughter. I know now that my parents' love was unconditional, but it didn't always seem like that to me growing up. I felt the need to earn their love by making the right choices, by never making mistakes. I needed to be indispensable, remember? My mother is a charismatic and astonishingly confident woman – the type of person who walks into a room and turns heads, making an instant impression. How could I ever measure up? I feared that I would never become the daughter, granddaughter, wife or mother everyone hoped I would be.

Don't get the wrong idea. Anxiety didn't stop me from functioning. On the contrary – I was *highly* functional. I had succeeded in the corporate world and at the same time was a mother to young children. I did those jobs well. I went to company events and social parties, danced on the dance floor, drank cocktails, laughed, wore the latest fashion trends, my hair and make-up always done to perfection. No one ever knew I was suffering inside because I had put up a thick veil that masked it. No one ever guessed.

So when I saw that question – What would you do if you weren't afraid? – on the wall at Facebook, I felt deeply moved. Throughout my life, anxiety had taken away the simple joys of life. It had stopped me from having joyful intimate relationships, from enjoying my job, from feeling good about myself. It had made me hide aspects of my personality and feel guilty and worried when I should have been content. The suggestion that I didn't have to live my life in a constant state of anxiety was almost inconceivable, and yet, here it was.

Of course, I'm not the only one to have experienced feelings of anxiety and despair, not the only one to have been ruled by them. In the US, it's estimated that more than one in ten adults are taking antidepressants or anti-anxiety drugs. Twenty per cent of the population are on some sort of psychiatric medication and doctors estimate that a further twenty per cent need to be medicated. There are fifty million prescriptions per year for Xanax, one of the more popular anti-anxiety drugs, alone. Other Western countries are not far behind. What is it about our times that leave so many people suffering from gnawing insecurities, ongoing frustrations, negative thoughts, despair and limiting self-doubt, while so many others feel empty and disconnected? Why is it that in our society, where more people than ever enjoy freedom and choice, it has become a struggle to feel happy?

The Search

Like many people, I had sought a solution for my anxiety in therapy and medication. My therapists explored my past – my childhood, and particularly my exposure to death. The Freudian model, on which they were trained, explains that mental illness is caused by events from our childhood. The focus is on the person's past and the assumption is that they will resist growth and change, instead relying on patterns formed in their earliest years. My father's job and the awful things I'd seen and heard, as well as the impact that the Holocaust had had on my family, were clearly – in my therapists' eyes – the causes of my anxiety. It was helpful, to a certain degree, to reflect on childhood memories, but at some point, after many years of therapy, I realised that the therapy wasn't going anywhere. We were revisiting the same stories, looking back through a blaming, limited lens.

Therapy became limited and limiting.

Don't get me wrong – learning that my feelings followed a textbook pattern really did help to normalise my anxiety. But reliving the things I'd seen in my past became a never-ending cycle. It felt like picking a scab, scratching the same wounds over and over again.

Even though at times the wounds healed a bit, my therapists only seemed interested in digging up again the horrors I'd been exposed to and what they termed the 'unfinished business' with my parents. It got to the point where hearing the phrase 'unfinished business' really triggered me. It didn't trigger me because I had unfinished business; it triggered me because I had actually resolved these issues after confronting my parents (which I talk about in greater detail in chapter two). Yet still the healing didn't come and still the pain was there.

After going to therapy for many years, things had actually gotten worse, not better. But although I declared to myself that I was ready to give up on living a joyful life, *deep inside me*, I knew there was something else, something bigger than my anxiety, a spark of hidden joy that I just couldn't get to. I didn't know what the spark I felt inside was or how to reach it, but I *believed* it was there. And every time I tried to voice these feelings or ideas to my therapists, they would respond in exactly the same tone, with exactly the same phrases: 'You are avoiding reality, Michal,' 'You're looking for an easy way out, Michal,' 'You are looking to suppress your real issues, Michal.' I realised my healing would not come from any therapist.

For a very short time, I turned to Buddhism. I read and educated myself, but I wasn't ready to embrace Zen practices and I wasn't able to let go of pain. Actually, I didn't *want* to let go of my pain or to avoid it – I wanted to look it in the eye, I wanted to solve it. I tried a life coach. One day he asked me if, given the choice, I would choose to cut out the 'anxiety part' of me, to remove it as if it had never been there. In all my years of therapy I had never been asked such a powerful question. Would I? Would I want to completely get rid of the uncomfortable aspects of myself? Would I erase a whole part of me?

After several long minutes of reflection, I realised that the answer was a definite NO! I still think about this moment often. It was a turning point for me with regards to the way I viewed my anxiety.

Even though I suffered daily, I wanted to keep every part of myself, even the painful parts. Who would I be without my life experience? Would I become a different person? Ultimately, this baggage was part of what made me *me*. I just didn't want to only look back. I wanted to look forward, too, to move towards something and find hope and potential. But I didn't know the way. I decided that, instead of trying to wipe away all these parts of me, I would learn to understand myself through a new lens, using a completely different perspective to Western psychotherapy. But what was that other perspective? I just didn't know.

It was around this time that I read a book by Viktor E. Frankl called *Man's Search for Meaning*. Dr Frankl was a gifted student of Sigmund Freud and a champion of psychoanalysis during its heyday in the 1920s. Frankl was a well-known neurologist, psychiatrist and therapist who challenged Freud's ideas. He started to disagree with Freud on a number of things, namely what really drives humans to act and think the way they do. For Freud, the fundamental human drives are pleasure and self-preservation. But Frankl saw that humans had something else – a yearning for meaning in their life. He began to develop a theory of psychotherapy called logotherapy, which means 'therapy of meaning'. Whereas

Freud believed that happiness comes from the pursuit of pleasure and the avoidance of pain, Frankl believed that the more we pursue happiness, the less likely we are to find it. Instead, we should view happiness simply as a side effect of finding something we care about. Happiness is not the goal itself – Frankl believed that humans are not simply seeking pleasure for its own sake, but are seeking meaning.

Dr Frankl came up with most of his findings during his time as a prisoner in the Nazi death camps where he was tortured, humiliated and nearly murdered on several occasions. He experienced incredible cruelty and was exposed to mankind's ability to commit terrible crimes against their fellow human beings. But Dr Frankl also made a groundbreaking discovery. He saw prisoners holding on to life, even when death would have been a relief.

But why? Why would someone want to survive, under horrific, hopeless, terrifying circumstances?

The answer he came up with was *purpose*.

What kept prisoners alive was their incredible internal drive to fulfil a unique purpose – a person to live for, a cause to support or a meaningful task to complete. There, in the horror of the concentration camps, Frankl discovered that finding purpose changes your outlook on life. It can even *save* your life.

This resonated powerfully with me, and not just because I had lived most of my life in the shadow of the Holocaust, hearing my grandparents' stories, feeling their fears. Frankl's ideas captivated me because I had already felt that small spark inside me and I knew that it was capable of growing into something more.

The Wisdom

And then it happened.

From the most unexpected place – a source I had never considered before – came a life-changing discovery: a powerful set of principles to better manage fear, anxiety, sadness and despair.

I discovered a guide to finding joy that I had never known about. A source of psychological wisdom that could help me when I felt stuck in life, that could show me how to find meaning and confidence.

I discovered Jewish wisdom.

It happened around the time of the Jewish festival of Passover, which celebrates the release of the Israelites from their years of slavery in ancient Egypt. Although I am Jewish by birth, I hadn't ever considered the meaning of Jewish holidays, in this case, Passover. However, that year, having decided to stop going to therapy because it was getting me nowhere, I remembered what a Jewish friend had said to me years ago when I asked her what Passover meant to her. She'd explained that Passover is the time of year when you remind yourself that although you're no longer enslaved in Egypt, you are still enslaving yourself to damaging things. You will always have 'your Egypt'. 'It's a reminder that you can get out of Egypt, but you can't get Egypt out of yourself,' she added.

At the time I had wondered what she meant, but now I started to understand the significance of the story. Egypt doesn't just mean a physical country. It symbolises any place where you are not free, where you are chained to something.

In Hebrew the word for Egypt is *mitzrayim*, which

means 'boundaries' or 'narrow straits'. I realised that the story of the Israelites' escape from Egypt isn't 'just' a historical story about liberation from slavery. It's a story that is lived every single day. It's the human story of liberating ourselves from narrowness, from our own personal restrictions, our own self-slavery. The fact that many of us are privileged enough to have physical freedoms to do whatever we want, whenever we want (within legal boundaries, of course), doesn't mean we are truly free. We can have *internal* chains – thoughts and self-beliefs – that keep us trapped, limited. What was I chaining myself to? What was I enslaved to that was making me feel so anxious? And how on earth could I set myself free?

As luck would have it, shortly after that Passover, I heard a talk by the Vice President of EMEA for Facebook, Lady Nicola Mendelsohn. She was being interviewed in the British press, sharing her career journey upon joining Facebook as their most senior leader outside of the US. She spoke openly about what most mattered to her in life: her four children, her charitable work and holding a senior position in the social media and advertising world so she can facilitate change. She also said that observing the Jewish day of rest, Shabbat, was central to who she was.

I was amazed. I had never heard of any other top executive who managed to combine a job with having four children, as well as being openly observant of religion. Was it really possible to fulfil my personal goals and be successful, while also finding myself spiritually? Here was Mendelsohn, openly sharing what some might consider to be her most vulnerable or weak points –

flexible working hours, having four children, the importance of religion in her life – and yet, all this only made her seem stronger in my eyes. Instead of trying to be a different person in each of the different settings of her life, she was simply herself in all of them.

It was Mendelsohn and the possibilities she represented that became part of my inspiration to join Facebook. Months later, as I stood in front of that question, I asked myself, 'What *would* I do if I weren't afraid?' And again, I felt the spark of something inside me, a tiny flame that was burning despite everything. I knew I was getting closer to discovery.

Later, I Googled 'depression, anxiety, finding happiness and' – although I wasn't religious – 'Judaism'. One of the first results pointed to the work of a Jewish professor of psychology in London and one of the leading academics in her field. Her name was Professor Kate Miriam Loewenthal. I decided to reach out to her. 'I suffer from anxiety and am looking for new therapeutic solutions,' I wrote. Having told her my story, I was surprised when she suggested I attend a class in Jewish spiritual texts taught by a Chassidic rabbi. 'A Chassidic rabbi?' I thought, 'What does Chassidic Judaism have to do with me?'

At the time, all I knew about Chassidic Judaism was that it's a religious Jewish movement that was established in the eighteenth century in eastern Europe. It was founded by a Polish rabbi known as the Baal Shem Tov. I have since learnt that Chassidic Judaism and its teachings, *Chassidut*, seeks to bring spirituality, joy and meaning to everyday life.

The way I embrace it, *Chassidut* teaches how to replace fear and anxiety with joy and purpose. It offers deep, yet down-to-earth and pragmatic teachings from the holy Jewish texts that can be applied to everyday life.

But at that point, my understanding of Judaism was limited. I had thought of it as a series of laws and rules that Jewish people were instructed to follow. I had never thought that what the Torah had outlined thousands of years ago could have anything to do with life today. My instinct was to be doubtful that Jewish texts could be a helpful resource for me. Still, something inside made me go.

I attended a class taught by Rabbi Mendel Gordon. We turned to an early work of Chassidic wisdom, first published in 1796, by Rabbi Shneur Zalman of Liadi. The book is called the *Tanya* and the wisdom it contains helps people like you and me find their purpose and bring spirituality into everyday life. It talks about the existence of the soul.

Transfixed, I read:

[The soul] is comparable to the flame of a candle which, by nature, continually flickers upwards, because a fire's flame is naturally inclined to detach itself from the wick... And even though by leaving its wick, and uniting with its source, the flame would be extinguished, and would cease to shine at all down here... nevertheless, this is what the flame is naturally inclined to do...
Tanya 19

And then I realised: the spark I felt inside me – that something I couldn't name or define – wasn't anything to do with my upbringing, my experiences or my thoughts. It was my *soul*. And this image of a flame, continually flickering, faltering, unceasingly trying to break free but always being held down, made me look at my anxiety differently. My inner angst was not a disease, nor was it some irredeemable damage I had picked up in childhood. *It was part of the human condition.* Like a flame, the soul can never be settled; it always flickers. My struggle, I thought, is really something quite beautiful: it is a symptom of always yearning to grow, like the flame which is pulled upwards. I wasn't a failure, I was just a beautiful flame.

Break Your Chains

My discovery of the hidden lessons of Jewish wisdom didn't happen overnight, but once I learnt about them, they changed the way I experienced life and helped me heal the most painful parts of myself. I am still the same person, but what I learnt allowed me to finally breathe, sleep and smile.

Instead of treating my anxiety and unhappiness as things I needed to completely get rid of, which is what I'd been trying to do my entire life, the Jewish ideas I was learning helped me control my thoughts and heal my heart. They allowed me to move forward, towards a joyful, confident life. Jewish wisdom showed me ways I could become a better version of myself.

I not only use Jewish wisdom in my personal life now, but also in my role as a leadership and culture consultant. It helps me to coach leaders to be better at their jobs and at their lives. I want to share these ideas because I truly believe that they can help you become more resilient, more courageous, more connected, more fulfilled and – most importantly – more yourself.

This is not a book on Jewish scripture; it is a book for anyone looking to find meaning and purpose, regardless of your personal background or faith. Jewish wisdom points out a great universal truth: that struggle is part of life. It's not a bug in the system. Life was designed this way. This *is* the system! And although it took me a long time to realise it, there *is* no life or growth without internal and external tension.

This book is not meant to convert you to religion. The principles I share come from Judaism, but they apply to people of all religions and none, to anyone who needs help. Ancient wisdom of course exists in many other cultures and religions, too. But the principles I focus on are the ones that resonated with me. They have helped me with my marriage, helped me solve conflicts at work, deal with teenagers at home, be a better mother, be a supportive sister, find meaning in my community, build and invest in friendships and cope with the inevitable juggle of commitments that is common to many women and men in the way we live now.

I don't know what pops into your head when you hear the words 'Jewish wisdom'. Maybe you're thinking, 'What does this have to do with me? I'm not Jewish.' Or maybe you are Jewish but not connected to or aware of the unique wisdom that lies within Judaism. Maybe when you think of Judaism, you imagine orthodox Jews who live a lifestyle so different to yours. Or maybe you are curious and think, 'What is this universal Jewish wisdom and how can it help *me* in *my* life?'

I invite you to be curious. Take that first step and

explore something you would never have expected to explore. Step out of your comfort zone. Who knows where it could lead? As Viktor Frankl said, 'When we are no longer able to change a situation, we are challenged to change ourselves.'

Self-reflection is the key to growth. So, too, is taking action, even if it is just one tiny step forward. One step at a time. I want to offer you a place for reflection and a way to 'take action' right here, in this book. I am going to end each chapter with a few coaching questions, titled 'If you change nothing, nothing will change'. Answer one question, answer two or answer them all, as long as you remain honest with yourself and make space for your personal growth.

As we embark together on the journey this book will take us on, ask yourself:

What would you do if you weren't afraid?
Excerpt from *Who Moved My Cheese?* by Dr Spencer Johnson,
(G. P. Putnam's Sons, 1988)

Setting Ourselves Free

We all have our own narrow straits that restrict us, stifle us, trap us. These internal chains of self-slavery – our own limiting thoughts and restrictive beliefs – might be what's making us afraid, what's keeping us from moving forward. But now it's time to break free.

2
FINDING YOUR FLAME

'From every human being there rises a light.'
The Baal Shem Tov

I'm sitting on a fake leather chair in a smart room in north London. I'm telling my therapist about the first time I saw a dead body.

'I was seven years old. We were living in the US, as my father was completing his residency in forensic pathology.'

The therapist nods.

'On Sundays my mother taught in a Hebrew school and my father would stay at home with me. I loved those mornings so much. We would watch TV together, *The Pink Panther* I think, and we would eat sweets. He would ask me about school and I would tell him the latest news. It was our special father-daughter time together. I remember him telling me one day how he'd felt when I was born. He said, "You were the most beautiful baby I have even seen. Your birth was a miracle." I remember thinking that I wasn't *actually* a miracle. But I guess it might have felt like that for my dad.'

'Why?' asks the therapist.

'Because every day he dealt with death.'

He makes a note and nods at me to go on.

'On one of these Sunday mornings I remember he had a call from the morgue asking him to come in urgently. It was something that couldn't wait. We had no family I could stay with and our neighbour, who used to babysit me, wasn't at home so he had to take me with him.

'When I entered the morgue it looked just like any other clinic, but I could tell that something was going on in the basement. I remember following my father to a room on the first floor with a big, boardroom desk. He gave me some paper and pens and asked me to wait there for him. It was sunny and warm outside and I felt safe. I knew my father had to work and I was happy to be with him.'

'And what happened then?'

'After a short while I got bored. I wanted to kno~~w~~ was going on in the basement. I walked down some s~~t~~ steps and at the bottom was a room where I saw a ma~~n~~ almost completely naked. He wasn't moving. He was lying on what looked like a metal stretcher. His face looked like he was in pain, his eyes were half closed and his mouth was open. I remember that his body was monstrously bloated – it looked like a giant balloon – and all over it were thick, white moving spots. I found out later that these were maggots. They grow on the skin when a person drowns and stays under water for a long time.'

'And how did you feel when you saw this?'

'Even at that age, I knew he was dead. I felt the ending of his life in my heart. I also, somehow, knew that his life had ended in an upsetting, tragic way.'

'And did you tell your father what you saw? That was a lot for a young child to take in, wasn't it?'

'No, I didn't. I wasn't supposed to be down there. He didn't want me to see it.'

'Michal, I wonder why you avoid conflict with your father. I think this unfinished business with him over what he exposed you to could be preventing you from developing healthy adult relationships.'

'But I wasn't angry with my father.' I say. 'What scared me the most was that I remember thinking, "Where are all that dead man's feelings now? His love for his family, his *entire life*? Is it just gone?" I couldn't believe that there wasn't something else, something that lived on.'

My therapist shakes his head. 'Michal, I wonder if you were thinking of that man's life as a defence mechanism to avoid your anger towards your father.'

This is a typical exchange I had with my (four!) therapists when I tried, as an adult, to live a fulfilled, joyful life. Not everybody's childhood was filled with morgues and autopsies like mine was, but then again, everyone has skeletons in their closets and their own painful memories. In my case, I found that with every memory I recalled, my therapists became more and more interested in the trauma I had been exposed to and the relationship I had with my parents. But they were less interested in my spiritual and emotional development – my internal need for growth.

My therapists were confident that they understood the root of my anxiety – after all, wasn't I a textbook case? They always wanted to hear more about my father. His job as a forensic pathologist fascinated them because it involved examining rape victims, babies and children who had been abused and all manner of other horrors that humans do to each other. When I wanted to move on from my childhood memories and talk about the present, my therapists seemed almost disappointed. They'd say I was avoiding the *real issues*. They'd conclude that my parents were the main reason for my difficulties and that I should confront them about the 'unfinished business' between us.

This approach naturally led me to put the blame at my parents' feet. How could they have exposed me to such horrors as a young child? How could they be so irresponsible, so unfeeling? I took action and confronted my parents. Then I took action and confronted my parents again. And again. I did so repeatedly and assertively. My dad accepted my anger. He acknowledged the situations where he had made bad judgements and he apologised for them. He explained that he sees death as a part of life, exactly the way that birth is, and that he didn't realise how scary it was for me. He asked for my forgiveness. I gave it. And so the 'unfinished business' was finished.

But it didn't feel good. These confrontations didn't improve my anxiety, they didn't make me feel any better. I still wasn't healing.

We Are (Not) Just Flesh

The Western, Freud-based form of psychotherapy my therapists had studied made me a particularly interesting subject for them.

To them, I was simply the sum of all parts of my childhood – a product of my conditioning. There was no room in their diagnosis for something unique, for my inner essence. And yet, I had always felt that there was something else in me. Even as my seven-year-old self looked at that man's corpse in the morgue, I felt that there was something to him in addition to the body I saw before me. I felt it enough to wonder where it had gone after his death.

Growing up, my maternal grandparents lived next door to us. They became sick and died not long after one another. I vividly remember thinking at the time that there was no way all the love I felt, all the other complex and unique emotions inside me, would one day disappear with my body. I even asked my father about the autopsies he performed and whether he thought the physical body contained another, 'little' body inside it that had all the feelings, memories and love. I asked if that smaller, invisible body was the part that never dies.

'No', he replied. 'We are just flesh.'

Unfortunately, my father's view was shared by all the therapists who treated me. When I went to university to study the psychoanalytic approach to team development, there was a statue of Freud right outside the building and, like Freud, that institution didn't talk about souls or feelings of love. It was purely clinical. Surgical. I use the word 'surgical' because Freud himself used the metaphor of the therapist as a surgeon. He wrote that the therapist should be like the surgeon, who 'puts aside all his feelings, even his human sympathy, and concentrates his mental forces on the single aim of performing the operation as skilfully as possible.' (*Recommendations to Physicians Practising Psychoanalysis*, 1912.) It's no wonder then, that the more therapy I had, the more I felt like one of my dad's autopsy patients. I was being cut open, layer by layer, and just like my dad had told me that there is nothing beyond the flesh, so did my therapists.

I do not want to sound like a therapy basher. I know that nowadays there are psychologists and psychiatrists who incorporate classic Freudian theory along with other schools of thought: mindfulness, Buddhism and meditation. But I've never met them. I also know that therapy is great for learning how to reflect, how to be curious about your life and how to take a moment to observe your life. But I found it to be so unyielding in its belief system. Funnily enough, Freud, in his later years, softened his approach to matters of faith and spirituality. While he remained an atheist, he wrote that having faith in God can lead to greater introspection and can help you break free from being a slave to the physical world.

Unfortunately, by the time Freud published these thoughts in one of his last books, *Moses and Monotheism*, his original ideas had become so firmly entrenched in the practise of psychoanalysis, that my therapists completely dismissed any talk of matters beyond the flesh.

I felt despair. At that point I believed that my past had scarred me forever, that my childhood experiences defined me and would continue to define me forever. I pretty much accepted that 'fact' and just hoped that things wouldn't get worse. But as I slowly began to discover the inspirational texts of Jewish wisdom, something promising and positive was evolving inside me. It was an understanding of the soul. I learnt that I carry much more than the sum of my life's events inside me. I have a soul – a 'spiritual flame' – which is my core essence. And the more it was hinted in therapy that I was *damaged for life*, the more I felt that positive flame growing inside me. For years I had been told that I was anxious because of all that I had seen, because of my parents' mistakes, because I wasn't ready to 'divorce' myself from my parents. But as I moved away from therapy and started applying Jewish wisdom to my life, I began to wonder, what if the key to understanding myself wasn't my past? What if the answers are in a completely different place?

The Breath of Life

Have you ever thought about who you were in the beginning?

You and I were born with something unique inside us. It's still there – it's our soul. And we are both on our own journey, a journey that started the moment we were born, or even before. And since we have a unique soul – our essence – who we really are is not just a product of our upbringing. Yes, of course, your upbringing and experiences have affected you and influenced who you are, but isn't there something much deeper and totally untouchable in you – in us – that was there before all that?

But what is the soul? And where does it come from?

The meaning of the word 'soul' in Hebrew – *neshama* – is related to the Hebrew word for 'breath'. That's because we first hear about the *neshama* when God created the first human, Adam. The Torah says:

> *And God formed man from the dust of the earth, and He blew into his nostrils the breath of life; and man became a living being.*
> Genesis 2:7

According to this verse, the human soul is, in effect, the breath of God. God made Adam's body and then, by injecting His own breath into it, brought the body to life. The concept of the *neshama* is that becoming alive and having a soul are the same thing. According to Jewish wisdom, every human originates from Adam and Eve. And therefore, every human has a body *and a soul*. Each of us contains a flame within us, a flame of God, a soul. And that flame needs to be nurtured and grown.

A Flame Within a Shell

Even during my therapy, I could feel there was something else inside me – that hidden spark that was capable of joy. Now I realise it was my soul. But why had I struggled for all those years to locate it? Why are we so unaware of this inner flame that we each hold inside? If I were to ask people whether they believe the soul exists, I think most would say yes. But if I asked them to describe their soul – to describe *their very own* soul – I think few would come up with an answer. We know the soul exists, yet we don't know much about it, and we don't really know how to look after it. We often feel the existence of our soul most strongly in times of difficulty. That's because when the soul isn't fulfilled, it sends us signals, calling for our attention, often through feelings of fear, sadness or anxiety.

But why is it so difficult to find the soul? Because the soul is encased inside a body. In Jewish mysticism there is a concept called *kelipa* (meaning 'shell'). The shell is a metaphysical barrier that obscures the soul and conceals the treasure within. The shell is associated with the mundane, with things that are not spiritual, such as money, work, success, popularity and beauty. These things have a very strong pull, and if we focus on them – and live for them – our happiness comes to depend on them. And so we experience fear: the fear of losing all these things.

But if we can see past the shell, past the distractions of the physical world, we might be able to find the divine energy within the shell, the divine soul within the body, that divine flame. The soul is oblivious to wealth, beauty and popularity. So too is it immune to the fear of failure, pain or rejection. The soul is eternal, spiritual. It seeks meaningful things like transcendence, growth, joy and fulfilment.

For me, the concepts of the soul and the shell underscore the way Jewish wisdom approaches the world: the physical world is an enabler, a material layer that covers the real purpose of life. I found this idea revolutionary. It made everything less frightening. And when I realised that my purpose was to somehow release and grow that flame within me, I saw what an important and deeply personal job we all have to do: we must get past that shell of fear and grow the flame inside.

Discovering that there was a powerful essence inside me when it felt like fear was taking over my life was a game changer for me. For years I had been disconnected from myself. I was focused on revisiting childhood trauma, letting others tell me what the problem was, living with the identity I had been labelled with, feeding my ego rather than my soul.

But your soul and your identity are not one and the same. Your soul existed in you before the influences of your upbringing or your culture, before you developed emotions and thought patterns. Your soul is beyond that. It doesn't come from your assumed feelings or beliefs; it was there way before.

We talk a lot today about 'finding yourself'. But it's important to differentiate between the identity that you 'wear' – the persona that you exhibit to the world – and the *essence of you*, which is your soul. You've developed your identity throughout your life and it's been shaped, affected and influenced by childhood experiences and the values you were brought up with. But deeper than your identity is your soul, the essence that was in you from the very beginning.

There is a relationship between the body and the soul: each has different needs but they are interdependent. I often think about the concept of 'self-care' – how it mainly focuses on the body. Taking time out, having a bath, doing exercise, eating healthy food – these are ways to care for yourself. But the soul needs self-care, too. The soul doesn't appreciate your attempts at a quick fix. A visit to the spa won't give it what it needs. It needs special care, understanding and attention. Every soul is unique. It needs to go on its own life journey and it needs you to fulfil its purpose and discover the reason it exists.

Where Are You?

Let's go back to Adam. You might remember the famous story from *Genesis* where Adam disobeyed God and sinned by eating the forbidden fruit. And after he sinned, Adam hid in shame. It's a familiar story, but now that I've been learning the concepts of Jewish wisdom, I look at it in a new light. Specifically, I learn from what God said to Adam, right after his sin, right after his failure.

The first thing God said to Adam after Adam ate the forbidden fruit was a question – the first question asked since humans were created. God asked: 'Where are you?' (*Genesis* 3:9) Did God not know where Adam was? Of course He did. God was really asking if *Adam* knew where he was, not physically, but existentially. Where on his journey was he right now? How far had he wandered from his potential?

You can see where I'm going with this. Where are *you*? Where is your soul? How deeply hidden beneath its fearful shell has it become? Are you being the person you have the potential to be?

What I find most interesting about the question of 'where are you?' is what God *didn't* ask. He didn't ask Adam, 'What have you done?' or 'What's wrong with you?' He didn't blame or accuse. His question was an invitation for self-reflection. It switched the focus from what Adam had done to who Adam was being.

This idea of moving away from blame and looking inwards at yourself is incredible. Let's think about how Adam was feeling: he was the first human to live, and the first to make a mistake. Can you imagine the pressure? And yet, no blame.

We all make mistakes. Some are small, some are colossal. And I'm sure we've all wanted to hide away in shame. We want to heal quickly, to recover from the disappointment and pain. For years I thought that something had gone 'wrong' in my life, that life was supposed to be perfect and that I or others had messed it up. But I was wrong. Messing up is part of life.

The idea that humans are *designed* to make mistakes is one of the fundamental concepts of Jewish wisdom. Life isn't about doing everything right, it's about the internal struggle and (hopefully) the lessons we learn for self-improvement. We are exactly the opposite of perfect: we are flawed and imperfect, ready to learn and improve ourselves and the world around us.

If we can ask ourselves, 'Where am I?', it might remove some of our fear. If we stop focusing on blame and start looking inside, finding the spark of who we were supposed to be, wouldn't it help us learn and progress on our personal journey?

In fixating on my past, picking over it endlessly in therapy, trying to make myself better by 'solving' my childhood, I had been asking the wrong question all along. I should have asked a different question: Where am I right now?

It's a question we all can – and should – ask ourselves. I also ask it of the leaders I coach in my professional life. It's not a question about what you've done or what's been done to you, but rather who you *are* and *where* you are on your personal growth journey – where is the real you that hides behind identity, labels and masks?

Often, all we know about ourselves are the bad things that have happened to us. And when we search for answers or healing, we tend to look backwards to those events. But if we ask ourselves not what has gone wrong, but *where* we are, and focus on *who* we are, we give the responsibility and power back to ourselves. It's not about what we've done, but who we have the potential to be. It's about *what can go right*.

Jewish wisdom tells us that our soul is our true essence, and searching for it, growing it, finding it beneath the shell, is the only thing that will allow us to control our fear and help us to become who we were meant to be.

One of my favourite Chassidic stories is about Rabbi Zusha of Anipoli, who once said, 'When I arrive at the gates of Heaven, I will not be asked why I wasn't Moses. I will be asked why I wasn't Zusha.' The message is so simple, yet so powerful. What matters most is that you fulfil your own unique potential, that you live as the soul and person you are meant to be. You are not supposed to be anyone else apart from yourself.

Soul

*Your soul is what makes you **you**. It is your essence, your unique, eternal, beautiful self. To nurture your precious soul, you must look past the superficial aspects of daily life and find your purpose.*

IF YOU CHANGE NOTHING, NOTHING WILL CHANGE

These ideas and the wisdom of the ancient Jewish texts may be very new to you, just like they were to me. The principles we've discussed so far are quite deep and different, aren't they? And they require reflection, and some time, to comprehend. In order to familiarise yourself more with their meaning and to assess how they could help you on your own journey, I invite you to answer one or all of the questions here. What's most important is to be deeply honest with yourself and to understand that, as Albert Einstein said:

'If you change nothing, nothing will change.'

1 What experiences and memories from your past have you been holding onto that you could slowly let go of? How could you slowly let go of them?

2 Imagine the flame inside you, your *neshama*, your soul. When do you feel it most? When was the last time you sensed it was trying to 'tell you something' about yourself? What was it trying to say? Close your eyes for deeper reflection.

3 Write down several words to describe your true essence – what's unique about your soul? What makes your internal flame evolve and grow?

4 Where are you – right now, in your life? Are you where you want to be? Are you being who you have the potential to be?

5 What, or who, if anything, are you hiding from? Why are you hiding and how could you get out of your hiding space?

3
REPLACE FEAR WITH PURPOSE

'The secret to a meaningful life is to do something outside yourself, something to repair tears in your community, something to make life a little better for people less fortunate than you.'
Ruth Bader Ginsburg

In his book *Man's Search for Meaning*, Viktor Frankl describes the terrible conditions he experienced during his time in Auschwitz and other death camps. He describes the guards' dehumanising treatment of the prisoners, the hard physical labour, the unsanitary conditions and how, every so often, someone would choose to take their own life by 'running into the wire' – the electric fences that surrounded the camp.

One day, one of Frankl's fellow prisoners told him that he was considering taking his own life. Frankl asked him, 'Why do you want to kill yourself?' The man said, 'Because I no longer have anything to expect from life.'

Under the circumstances, this man's answer might be considered understandable: what could life possibly hold for him now that the world as he'd known it had ceased to exist, not to mention the loss of his family and home? But Frankl didn't see it this way. He looked at his friend and told him honestly, 'It might be the case that you have nothing to expect from life. But isn't it conceivable that life expects something of you?'

When I read this story, I was moved by Frankl's attitude of hope. I read it long before the day I attended that first *Chassidut* class. And then, after I had started learning about Jewish wisdom, I discovered that Rabbi Shneur Zalman, author of the *Tanya*, told a similar story about a businessman who suffered terrible financial losses and was unable to pay his bills. He came to the rabbi and complained bitterly that he no longer had the money he needed. But instead of commiserating with him, the rabbi saw his predicament differently. He said, 'I'm hearing a lot about what you need. But have you ever considered what you are needed for?'

In my desperation to 'fix' myself I, like many others, had become so concerned with what I needed to get out of life that I had forgotten about what I had to give. I hadn't realised that, just as I had a unique soul inside me, I also had a unique purpose. My job was not to only see what life could give me, but to see what I could give to others. Where modern culture says, 'How can I be fulfilled?', Jewish wisdom asks, 'What am I here to do?'

In my role as a leadership and workplace culture coach, what I find most interesting about the hundreds of professionals I've coached over the last twenty years is that many of them spend little or no time learning about themselves. They invest time into analysing other companies, understanding market trends, managing change and leading others, but they don't prioritise reflecting upon their own passions, what inspires or uplifts them and what they're here to do. I also see many leaders and managers who, despite the successful career they display to the outside world, are feeling empty and lost inside. I was familiar with that feeling, too. Superficially, I had so much to 'celebrate'. Even regarding meaningful things, I had plenty to be grateful for. Yet I would wake up in the morning and ask myself, 'Am I missing something? Is this really what life is all about?'

Frankl calls this emptiness the 'existential vacuum'. He describes an internal void that comes about when you cannot clarify what is truly meaningful to you. This void of meaninglessness causes anxiety, sadness and a lack of purpose. He explains that, 'These days no instinct tells you what you need to do, and no tradition tells you what you ought to do; sometimes you don't even know what you wish to do. Instead, you end up doing what other people do or what other people tell you to do.' We feel lost. Even when we are living what looks like a beautiful life, with financial stability, a good job, surrounded by people who love us, we still feel the existential vacuum.

The existential vacuum is a crisis in which people cannot find meaning and purpose in life. It's that gut-wrenching feeling that makes you feel purposeless, as if deep inside, you know there's more you should be doing – but you don't know what it is. And that feeling – that life is meaningless – often results in you seeking immediate satisfaction: something that will fill up the emptiness inside. Anything to avoid that terrible void.

There was a point in my career when I was totally disengaged from my workplace. I would go to work and do my best, achieve all my goals and perform at the highest level. But inside I felt like I had no purpose. I wanted to *do* something, to create, to leave my mark on the world, but I didn't feel like I was accomplishing any of those things at work. I looked around at my friends and my professional community, and I saw that some of them had founded their own companies. They seemed successful and rewarded. Instead of figuring out what my purpose was and following it, I focused on my ego, on wanting to look successful, too. So what did I do? I decided to start my own company, of course.

In retrospect, I didn't start a company because I had a passion for a specific product or service, or because I could see what good this company would do for its employees, clients or the world. My main motivation stemmed from the misguided belief that if I appeared successful, I would feel successful. Clearly, I was trying to fill that increasing void I felt. I decided that it would be a tech startup, not because I'm that tech savvy, but because it seemed like something with which others were finding success. I had a good idea for a product and I began building the business model. I started working on a business plan and set up meetings with potential partners and investors. I even managed to get a few investors interested. But increasingly, I found these meetings a drag. I dreaded yet another round of discussions about finance and development and I would find myself avoiding working on it.

It was only when Yair my husband asked me one night, just before I went to bed, 'Remind me, Michal, why are you starting this company?' that I realised I was on someone else's journey, not my own. I was focusing on my ego instead of on my true purpose, and I was on a fast track to yet more emptiness and dissatisfaction.

Fill Yourself with the Right Things

One of the most important lessons I learnt from Jewish wisdom is that feeding the ego is the quickest way to starve the soul. When we do things because they seem impressive or make us look successful, we are missing our chance to pursue our true purpose. We are focusing on the shell instead of the divine energy and the soul. But when we stop looking at life as something that should always satisfy us, and instead focus on what we could do for others, we get closer to finding the meaning we were looking for all along. Jewish wisdom encourages us to look at our emptiness through a totally different lens and see that what we feel as emptiness is not emptiness after all: it is actually a void that is being filled with the wrong things.

There is a concept in Judaism called *bittul*. *Bittul* is a Hebrew word with no straightforward translation, but in this context it means 'selflessness'. The practice of *bittul* is an attempt to empty yourself of your *self* to make space for the divine. In other words, freeing yourself from yourself. It requires a combination of modesty, humility and selflessness. In a world where most self-help books advocate self-care and 'me-time', this could sound quite counterintuitive (at least, that's what I thought before I truly understood). How can emptying yourself help you find fulfilment?

Bittul or selflessness isn't saying that you don't matter. It doesn't mean that a person's life, feelings and experiences aren't important – they most certainly are. Selflessness teaches us that being full of yourself and caring only about yourself, obsessing over what you need to do to *make yourself feel better all the time*, is often exactly what's getting in the way of living a purposeful life. The idea of selflessness is that, in order to grow, you have to make space inside for something that isn't just about you. It's a mindset shift from 'I am everything' to 'I am *not* everything'. When I focus only on myself – my looks, my talents, my failures, my achievements, my mistakes, my success, my popularity, what I need, what I want – I can become depressed and afraid. But when I focus on how I can utilise my talents, my achievements – even my failures – for the benefit of others, then I start to feel more fulfilled.

This is actually a new way of looking at Frankl's existential vacuum. I like the idea that the vacuum isn't emptiness at all. It comes from being too full – of ourselves.

Once this new understanding takes shape, the solution, according to Jewish wisdom, is not to add *more* – not to endlessly chase personal satisfaction – but to take away. We must understand that our role on Earth isn't just about making the most out of life for ourselves. It's about finding out what we can do for others. Crucially, the two don't contradict each other. In fact, they go hand in hand. You will feel great power, energy and joy once you figure out how to combine what you need with what is needed of you.

I didn't know it at the time, but I'd experienced this concept for the first time as a teenager. Although I did well at school and had a nice group of friends, I felt anxious and lost. I wanted 'more' but didn't even know what would make me 'happy'. I felt lonely inside. I was probably looking for meaning but didn't know what it was.

A friend of my mother's, who had a PhD in social work, told me there was much I could do. She had founded a women's shelter that was not too far from where I lived but was of course kept secret so the abusive partners of the women there would not be able to find it. The shelter was a safe place for the women and their children, but there was always a risk that a disgruntled husband would show up, so secrecy was extremely important. She suggested that I become a 'big sister' to one of the children, and take them out of the shelter once or twice a week. And though I was afraid (those were my worst years of fear and anxiety), for some reason, I said, 'I'll do it.'

For a few years I was a 'big sister' to a beautiful girl, inside and out, who lived with her mother at the shelter. A girl who had seen the worst, in life and in men. A girl who needed time away from the enclosed environment of the shelter, with all its reminders of violence and fear. She waited all week for our Friday excursions – trips to a nearby shopping mall or walks in the park. But soon enough I realised that *I* needed those Fridays just as much. Those Fridays changed me. They gave me meaning, they gave me perspective, they were more *real* than anything else in my life at that point. And the reason it was so meaningful to me was because I didn't think of 'me' but rather, shifted the focus to someone else.

Although selflessness in search of a higher purpose is a Chassidic concept, I've found it relevant in all areas of my life. I've used it to help leaders of large corporations shift their focus from what it is that *they* need, to what they are needed *for*. And through the process of asking what needs they could 'empty' themselves of, they are often able to discover the needs they might fulfil for others.

A Tale of Two Pockets

The Hebrew alphabet is made up of twenty-two letters. Jewish wisdom teaches that the letters themselves, and the combinations in which they are used, are deeply meaningful and contain great wisdom. One such example is the word 'me' or 'I', which in Hebrew is *ani*. It consists of three letters: Aleph, Nun and Yud. The same three letters can be rearranged to form the word *ain*, which means 'nothingness'. Does that mean we are nothing?

As shocking as it may sound, the answer is sometimes… yes. Sometimes we are nothing. But we are also something. In fact, we're both – everything and nothing.

Before you write off this concept which sounds a bit contradictory, give me a moment to explain. There is a Jewish concept that every human being is an entire world:

> *He who saves a life... it is as if he saved an entire world.*
> Mishna Sanhedrin 4:5

Yet Jewish thought also tells us that we are 'nothing' and that we are here to serve a greater purpose than just fulfilling our own selfish needs. Confusing, right?

I once heard a story that helps visualise and resolve this apparent contradiction. Rabbi Simcha Bunim, a Polish Chassidic leader at the turn of the nineteenth century, advised his community on how to live with this duality. He said, 'Everyone should have two pockets, with a note in each to use when necessary. One note should say, "The world was created for me," and the other the words, "I am but dust and ashes."'

When I first heard this, I wasn't sure how I felt about it. Why should I consider myself 'dust and ashes'? Why would anyone choose to think of themselves as dust? It took some thought to understand the deeper meaning of this message. One of the greatest internal tensions we experience is finding the balance between thinking about 'me, myself and I' and thinking about ourselves in the service of others. If you compare how many times a day you say 'me' with how many times you say 'you', what do you discover? Which do you say more? Today more than ever we are encouraged to think about ourselves – about achieving results, succeeding, reaching targets, wanting to be visible, wanting to be admired. We are advised to dream big, to want more, to live life to its fullest. And there is nothing wrong with that – as long as we *also* develop the ability to practise humility and serve a greater cause than just ourselves.

The idea isn't to reduce ourselves to dust. Dust and ashes represent healthy humility. And they remind us that it's not just about us. Thus we are 'nothing' on our own, but we are everything when we serve others and a higher cause.

I actually found the idea of Rabbi Bunim's two notes to be highly practical in helping me find balance and perspective. I liked this idea so much that I have literally written out the two notes! I like to keep them accessible for the right moments. Let me share how this has helped me navigate some everyday life situations.

A couple of years ago I had a disappointment at work. I didn't get a promotion that had been promised to me. I'd put in years of hard work with good results, but, in the end, I didn't get it. My ego was hurt. I felt low, even betrayed. And then I realised that I should be doing exactly the opposite of focusing on my ego. I chose to take out the 'dust and ashes' note. Oddly enough, it provided some comfort. It reminded me I was not the centre of the universe after all. There were other talented colleagues who also deserved recognition. And maybe – just maybe – I wasn't as good as I thought I was. Reading that I was like dust and ashes helped me let go and remove myself from the centre for a while.

But I had use for the other pocket, too. When I first started thinking about writing this book (it wasn't my idea by the way!) it totally took me out of my comfort zone. I had never written a book before, let alone in a language that wasn't my mother tongue. Also, it would cover principles I'd only started learning about seven years ago. I asked myself, 'Who do you think you are, Michal, that you could actually write a book? What are your credentials? Why would anyone read what you have to say?' I was about to give up on the whole crazy idea when I realised I was feeling a lack of confidence in my own abilities. So I pulled out the note that said the world was created for me. It reminded me that if I truly believed in the power of Jewish wisdom and its ability to improve people's lives, then I had an opportunity – a mission – to share it. And only I could write this specific book the way I envisioned it. I decided that I *would* write the book, that it *would* happen, and that this would be my purpose.

I can only speak for myself, but I know that for a very long time, I filled myself with the wrong things. I sometimes still do. It takes time and practice to regulate this. Selflessness is not a shortcut, an overnight transformation. It's a way of living, and it requires daily work and a real commitment. But... it's in our hands. How amazing is that? The solution to one of the biggest emotional problems many of us face, the existential vacuum, is something we can find and reach for ourselves. And we can start right now, by asking a new question:

What am I needed for?

Find Your Purpose Through Your Strengths

One way to start finding your purpose is to discover your strengths. You need to investigate what activities make you feel content and strong. There is no benefit in trying to copy someone else's purpose, even if it looks cool or impressive. I learnt that when I started my own company for the wrong reasons. In the same way that your soul is unique, so are your passion and purpose.

When I work with leaders on finding their strengths, I take a totally different approach to what you'd imagine. I don't focus on what they are good at. I base my discovery journey with them on uncovering who they were originally supposed to become, what their true essence is all about. I don't spend time asking them about their school years or their 'achievements'. Rather, I ask them to tell me about a time in their life when they felt they were doing exactly the right things – when they felt strong. I use the definition of 'strengths' as detailed in Marcus Buckingham's book *Now, Discover your Strengths*. According to Buckingham, strengths are the things you do that make you feel stronger. They are the things that, when you do them, they make you feel *in flow*, as if you were born to do these activities. They feel natural to you. Most often you'll be good at them, but not always. What matters is how you feel when you do them: strong.

It's helpful to think about your strengths in the context of your personal and professional life. Often they will correlate. In my personal life, I get energy and feel *in flow* when I can help my family and friends grow and feel fulfilled. I feel the same flow when I develop a company's culture or help build strong teams. This is my strength.

That's why, when I was offered the opportunity to join TikTok as Europe's company culture lead, I just couldn't resist. I loved my work at Facebook and deeply identified with the organisation, but when I was offered an opportunity to help shape and build a company culture, to paint a white canvas with meaningful colours of inclusion, care and growth, it appealed to me so much. It was the perfect opportunity to exercise my strengths: coaching and helping others to find their meaning. This is what I was born to do.

When one of my children arrives back from school looking a bit down or confused and says, 'Mum, something happened at school and I need to talk it through,' or when a friend calls and says, 'Michal, I feel unhappy in my current job and I'm ready for a change. Can you help me?' – these are the moments that bring me to life. My concentration and energy levels go sky high and I am ready to focus solely on that person. I also feel fulfilled when I am asked to get involved in solving a relationship conflict.

My strengths are feeling comfortable with the uncomfortable, solving problems and talking about the really important things. So much so that at work and among my friends, I am known as 'The Elephant Caller'. If there's something that everyone can feel but no one wants to be the first to mention, it's most likely me who will bring it up. I don't want there to be an elephant in the room. I don't look for tension, but once it's there and it's getting in the way, I will be the one to call it out as a way to start a meaningful conversation.

Identifying and sharing your strengths with others is not blowing your own trumpet. It is important to know what you love doing and what you are good at doing. This can get you closer to finding your purpose. Knowing your strengths will lead you to study the right subject, join the right workplace, find the right job and even date the right people.

Think about your family, friends, job and community.

What are the things that you do with them or for them that make you feel strong, *in flow*, as if you are doing 'your thing'?

If you carefully and curiously look at the world around you and the dynamics you have with your family, community and colleagues, you will find that signals about your purpose arise every once in a while. Sometimes you discover what your purpose is *not* as part of the journey towards discovering what it *is*. For example, sometimes you really want something, or think you 'deserve' something, but you don't get it – a promotion at work, dating a certain person, being invited to an exclusive event. If you find yourself getting frustrated, angry or hurt because it's not going 'your way', pause for a moment and ask yourself honestly, 'Am I forcing something that isn't right for me? Am I going against a path or purpose that was never mine to take?'

Some of life's toughest moments are about accepting things that weren't meant to be – a relationship, a job, a house move, a life project – things that we may desperately want but are simply not for us. Accepting this is painful at times and yet, we all must go on our unique journey. If events are telling you that certain things are not yours to have, maybe it's time to move forward, without fear, and discover what you are here to do.

Accepting the fact that you can't fully control your life – your relationships, career, health, ageing – is one of the greatest ways to manage fear. (And one of the hardest things to accept. Believe me, I know.) When you accept that some things are out of your control, you realise that all you can do is try your best to become the person you have the potential to be.

Fill Emptiness with Purpose

When we talk about life's 'purpose', it's important to know that we're not talking about one big, dramatic life mission, that if you miss it you've failed at life. Discovering your purpose is a journey that takes time. Committing to living your purpose doesn't mean you will suddenly discover it. Purpose doesn't work like that. As you go through different phases and situations in life, your purpose will change, as will you. Remember – no one is watching you. You don't need to share your life's purpose on social media or announce it to the world. Your mission is to discover your purpose(s) throughout your life, and then, most importantly, to act on it.

You might have already discovered your current purpose, or you might not yet know how to find it. I strongly believe that we are in this world to do good and our task is to be open and curious to discover our role here, at this moment in time. When we find our purpose, we acknowledge that there is a higher meaning to our life. And when that happens, the things we worry about – money, jobs, beauty, success, social acceptance – are put into perspective.

There is a saying, attributed to the Baal Shem Tov: 'Perhaps a soul comes to Earth for seventy or eighty years only to do a favour for another in need.' Maybe your purpose here on Earth is just that – to do a single meaningful thing for another person. Whatever your purpose is, finding it will hopefully be a step towards reducing your sense of despair, fear or anxiety, and replacing it with purpose.

Selflessness

Selflessness is the practice of internal reflection in which one empties oneself of ego and purely selfish thoughts, in order to connect with a higher reality. It is not self-annihilation. On the contrary, it is a state of transcendence. It asks that you fill yourself with meaningful thoughts and actions to lift you up beyond egocentric focus. Use this method of self-nullification to remember that not everything is about you. Empty your heart and mind of unhelpful thoughts and try to 'fill' yourself with the right things: meaningful, purposeful things. This will feed your soul and help you overcome fear and despair.

IF YOU CHANGE NOTHING, NOTHING WILL CHANGE

Finding your purpose at this moment of your life and discovering what is truly meaningful to you right now is rarely a simple task. As we said before, your purpose will change and evolve, the same way you do as a person. Whether you are exploring your purpose already, or not, the questions below could help you focus on what is meaningful for you, right now. Answer one, two or all of the questions. No one is watching. Just be honest with yourself – you don't need to impress. You only need to be real.

1 At this point in your life, what gives you most meaning?

2 What activities or thoughts make you feel *in flow*, in your element?

3 Think about the idea that your 'strengths' are those activities that make you feel strong.
What are your 'strengths'?

4 What unhelpful thoughts, beliefs, behaviours or actions can you empty from yourself?

5 What purposeful thoughts, beliefs, behaviours or actions could you be filling yourself with? How will they help you live more meaningfully?

4
CROSS YOUR NARROW BRIDGE

'My mother always used to say,
"Don't just sit around and complain
about things. Do something."
... So I did something.'
Kamala Harris

One of my earliest childhood memories is sitting on my grandmother Chana's lap, in her wheelchair, and listening to her stories. Other grandmothers told stories of castles and fairies, but my grandmother told stories about the Holocaust. I loved her stories and would beg her to tell them, even though I knew them by heart.

The story she told me most often was from the early 1940s in Poland, when Chana, aged twenty-nine, had lost touch with her family and was forced by the SS (the Nazi military police) onto a train with thousands of other captured Jews. Crushed between dozens of people, thirsty and sick, she didn't know where she was going. As she struggled to breathe, it hit her – something very bad was about to happen, something worse than anything she had experienced so far in the war. She knew instinctively she had to get off the train.

She found a crack in the train that at first looked way too small for her body, but she managed to squeeze herself through. The train was going so fast. It was the moment of truth. She forced her body through the boards – and jumped!

Chana injured both legs as she hit the ground. She heard her ribs crack. The Nazis were shooting after her as she limped away and hid in a field. After night fell, she dragged herself to a farm and found shelter in the pig barn. She found out later that the train had been going to the concentration camp at Auschwitz.

I would listen to my grandmother tell this story with great admiration but also great fear. I knew the reason she shared this horror with me was to prepare me for life, to build my own survival instinct. 'This could happen again,' is what she used to say. For the first fifteen years of my life I dreamt about the Nazis. I would imagine the soldiers' boots and the sound they had made in my grandmother's village when the soldiers murdered her parents, Moshe and Miriam Arbitman, and her sister, Bluma. I dreamt about the big Nazi eagle flying at full speed towards my bed and kidnapping me, taking me all the way from Israel to Auschwitz. Most mornings I'd wake up terrified in my bedroom in Tel Aviv. The moment it took to realise that it was only a bad dream felt like forever.

Everything worried me. I would wake up in the middle of the night and check that my parents were breathing. I became obsessed with the pain and suffering of the world, and felt guilty about enjoying myself. How could I enjoy the pleasures of life when there were so many tragic things happening out there? What if my actions would cause harm? I became a people pleaser, wanting to make everyone happy and doing everything in my power to stop things from going wrong.

As an adult, I carried with me not only anxiety but a sense of heaviness. Looking back, I can see that I felt as if I was responsible for everyone and everything. At times, I was literally paralysed by these feelings. Once, early in my marriage, my husband Yair and I were lucky enough to take a trip to Paris. For some reason, being away from home put me off balance. I found myself lying in my hotel bed, my heart beating fast, my whole body hot. I couldn't leave the room. I was having a full-blown panic attack, and while I was mortified that my husband had to see me like that, more than anything, I was infuriated with myself: I was exactly the same age as my grandmother when she jumped off that train. But while she'd lost so much and was at risk of losing her life, I'd just married a wonderful, kind man and moved to London, a new place full of great opportunities. I was supposed to be happy! I remember thinking, 'What is wrong with me?'

Replace Fear with Action

A few years after the Paris incident, while fear was still controlling my life, I was walking home from my London underground station one Friday afternoon. Friday evenings have been hard for me since leaving my homeland. In Israel, there is a special energy on Friday evenings, before the sunset which marks the beginning of the holy day of Shabbat. It's in the air: a sense of holiness, an invitation to transition into a different mode. At this point, I didn't practise Shabbat, or think of it in a spiritual way, but I still felt like I was missing something on Friday nights. I felt a yearning for something, though I didn't know what it was.

On this particular evening, the sun was going down and I could smell the subtle change in the air that marks the shift from winter to spring. The skies were orange and it was quite mild. I was annoyed with myself. Such a gorgeous evening and I still couldn't shake my depression, my fear. Suddenly, I heard a group of young men singing a song that made me slow down, until I froze. It was a song I had heard many times before. I'd heard it as a child growing up in Israel. It is part of the Jewish culture. And yet it felt like I was hearing the words for the first time, as if those young men were singing especially for me.

It is called *Gesher Tzar Me'od* and this is how it goes:

The whole world is a very narrow bridge,
a very narrow bridge,
a very narrow bridge.
And the main thing is to have no fear,
to have no fear at all.

That evening, these familiar words touched me. Yes, the world *is* a very narrow bridge. My internal world was terrifying – life stretched out before me like a steep, unconquerable path, like a bridge too narrow to cross. How could one have no fear at all? The song wasn't just asking me to learn to cope with my anxiety. It was asking me to have no fear *at all*.

I later learnt that the words that inspired this song were written towards the end of the 1700s, by a rabbi called Rebbe Nachman of Breslov. Rebbe Nachman was a great Chassidic leader who lived in a very difficult time. He suffered physical and emotional pain, and the Jewish community he led in Breslov (Bratslav), Ukraine, was the victim of poverty, anti-Semitism and pogroms. After many years of suffering he realised that there was not much he could do about the realities of life, but what he could do was change himself and help his community to do the same.

Rebbe Nachman took little-known principles from the Torah and turned them into daily practices. And with this short and simple song, he gave his followers a treasured piece of Jewish wisdom: that even in difficult, fear-inducing situations, they should face that fear, and power through it without hesitation. This is Rebbe Nachman's message: everyone should move forward, always, and cross their personal bridges. No looking back.

For years I had been paralysed by my fear. It seemed that no matter what I tried, I couldn't get rid of it, and if I couldn't be rid of it, what else could I do? Rebbe Nachman's song gave me the answer: anxiety won't be solved by standing still. There is another option: to move forward. I needed to replace fear with action.

A little dose of fear isn't bad, it can keep us safe. But when fear becomes paralysing, when it holds us back, then we need to move beyond it. Instead of just talking and thinking about my anxieties, I must also act.

Personally, my life would have turned out very differently if I hadn't taken a leap of faith every now and then. I think the perfect example is how I came to live in the UK. I was nearly thirty at the time and had finished my master's degree. I was working at a leading organisational development consulting firm and my career path as a leadership consultant looked promising. I loved my job, I had family and friends around me and the thought of moving abroad had never crossed my mind.

I also had a boyfriend – Yair. Yair wanted to study for his MBA in London. The idea, when he brought it up, sounded frightening. It would mean starting all over again. I had a great job in Israel, and I couldn't imagine being able to have a similar career elsewhere. People said things were very different in London and, with no local experience, I was told, my chances of a successful career were slim.

But I loved Yair and wanted to have a life together

with him. In fact, I thought it was high time we got married (an idea *Yair* found frightening). Despite my insecurities, I did believe in myself. I believed I could make it anywhere. London too.

We ended up taking a double leap of faith: we got married and moved to London a few days later. I did have to begin all over again. I started out as a receptionist at a spa. I learnt the local culture and improved my English – I even grew to understand the various local accents. Slowly I climbed the career ladder (again). It wasn't easy, but my leap of faith worked out for me in the end.

(It worked out for Yair, too. Marrying me was the best decision of his life. Ask him, and he'll tell you. And if he is only saying it out of fear, that's fine. As I said before, a little dose of fear is okay...)

So you see, taking that leap was a way for me to replace fear with action. But sometimes, when fear paralyses us, there isn't an obvious step to take. Sometimes, we can't see a clear way forward. Later, when I'd become familiar with Jewish wisdom, I learnt that often just *doing* is the only way to get past the fear, the only way to change how we think and feel.

But doing what? Well, this is where it gets interesting. There is a Jewish idea that action can in fact precede understanding. That doing something – anything – is the first step. Purpose will follow. There are times in life when we need to take a leap of faith into the unknown, a first step on the very narrow bridge. When we choose courage over fear, when we choose action, we choose to live instead of just exist.

Pause Thinking, Start Doing

It isn't surprising that Jewish wisdom promotes action. It's in the DNA of the Jewish faith. In Judaism, you are encouraged to act, to take a leap of faith.

I find this to be one of the most inspiring Jewish principles. I'm not suggesting you commit yourself to things without knowing what you're signing up for – taking unnecessary risks is unwise and can even be dangerous. But I do wonder if our generation follows the very opposite of this principle. I worry that we over analyse rather than act. Why are we so hesitant to act? Do we really expect life to come with full guarantees and assurances? Is it reasonable to expect to maximise every opportunity, and if we can't then to avoid taking action altogether? Life isn't perfect, nor should it be. Life is about trying, about making a move. There might be nothing to lose by acting first and then growing into learning, into understanding, into solving.

Looking back to when I first started studying the principles of Jewish wisdom, I am reminded of a Friday evening when I carried out just such an action. It was a different Friday evening to the one when I was stopped in my tracks by the words of that familiar song. I had just started attending synagogue, and a kind woman gave me a set of Shabbat candles. I had mixed feelings about this. I had no desire to observe the holy day of Shabbat. And yet I remembered what I had read in that first class with Rabbi Gordon – that the soul was like the flame of a candle. For some reason I had the inexplicable urge to do what my ancestors have done for many thousands of years.

So one Friday night I lit the candles. I did not know why I was doing it – I didn't even understand much about Shabbat, yet I decided to light the candles anyway. The first two Fridays I felt very little – I just watched the candles and reflected on the week that had passed. But after the third week of lighting Shabbat candles in the traditional way, just before sundown on Friday night, and reciting the holy blessing, I realised that I could feel a connection – to myself and to my heritage.

Sometimes just *doing* without over thinking is the only way to move forward towards joy, fulfilment and meaning. The act itself helps us move past the fear and, in some instances, it is the only way to change how we think. Ask yourself, 'What's the worst that could happen?' What risk am I taking by saying yes to a job, or a date, or a course? That the job might not work out, the date won't go so well or the course might not be as interesting as I thought? That's the very nature of opportunities: they come and they go, and you cannot guarantee success. Don't fear them, take them.

Crossing the Bridge of Trust

Trust, between friends, family or co-workers, is an example of a narrow bridge that so many people find hard to cross. Think about it: when you trust someone, by definition you don't *know* that they are trustworthy, you just *trust* that they are. It is hard to get over the fear that someone will let you down. Yet, despite this inherent uncertainty, we all depend on trust in our daily lives, at home and at work. It is the very foundation of every relationship, and of teamwork.

Effective teamwork is one of the most critical factors in company success. Historically, companies invested in upskilling and training for managers and leaders only, but in recent years there has been a growing shift to investing in teams.

I have been fascinated by 'teamwork' since my army service. In the army, one's team, the army unit, becomes like family. My best friends are the young women who were in my team in the army nearly thirty years ago (gulp!) They are my sisters. Of course, like in every family, there is sometimes conflict, tension and even anger. But above all, there is mutual trust. Company teams are not so different.

Patrick Lencioni is one of the leading thinkers in the field of teamwork. In his book, *The Five Dysfunctions of a Team*, he highlights trust as the most fundamental element needed for effective teamwork. Without trust, a team will never fulfil its potential to be as effective as it can be (and I would add that the same applies to families).

But what do we do once we discover that there is low trust or no trust at all within a team? How do we cross the bridge of building trust and move towards a trusting team? And do we really have to talk about trust? It feels uncomfortable; it risks conflict.

One of my most memorable coaching experiences was with a senior leadership team that was described by its leader as 'dysfunctional'. Its members were polite to one another, they even laughed at each other's jokes, but they didn't share information with each other and they didn't include each other in critical decision making. The HR business lead, who I partnered with, shared her frustration, saying, 'I can't put my finger on why they're not working well together. It's as if they're avoiding something, as if there's some tension between them that's getting in the way of healthy teamwork.'

'Great,' was my immediate reaction. 'Let's ask them exactly that – what's in your way as a team, what's the elephant in this team?'

And so we got the team together.

'Are you currently the best version of this team?' I asked them. 'Are you fulfilling your potential as a team?' One after the other they shook their heads. I suggested an exercise. I asked them to take a piece of paper and write down in clear capital letters an answer to this question: 'What is standing in the way of the team working better together?'

And here is what I read out from the twelve pieces of paper, one after another:

Trust, Trust, Trust, Lack of clear direction, Trust, No direction, Trust, No clarity on goals, Trust, Trust, No clear strategy and... Trust.

After hearing what sounded like a jury's verdict, the room was silent. It was an uncomfortable silence, but I also sensed relief. That's it – the elephant was out there.

And so we started talking about why there wasn't any trust. They brought up events from years before, as well as more recent ones. One member was very upset. They asked for more time. We extended the meeting.

'How can we build trust?' one of them asked me. 'What do we need to do now?'

I explained that trust is tricky. Trust is like love: you know straight away if it's there or not, but it's incredibly difficult to build. It takes a lot of time and care to establish trust, yet it can be destroyed in the blink of an eye. The first step is to have faith in your ability, as a team, to build trust together. That forms the basis of your team. To *choose* to *believe* that you will 'get there' together, and that each of you has a critical role to play. Choosing to believe in your team is that first step on the narrow bridge.

Don't Be Afraid of Failure

When I worked at Facebook I loved the motto, 'Fail harder.' It's certainly an unusual motto, one that evokes the shadows of what we are always most afraid to do: make a mistake, be wrong. Flat out fail. But this motto is what ensures that employees don't fear launching new solutions and designing new products. It breeds innovation. No one wants to make mistakes, but personal and company growth isn't possible without being bold, going all the way, trying new things and, yes, getting it wrong a few times along the way. Allowing and even encouraging its employees to fail harder is Facebook's way of replacing fear with action. Don't be afraid of making mistakes, just go for it, cross that bridge!

People often think of action as something they need to do in front of others, as if they need to be 'seen' doing, acting. But I have come to see things very differently. The greatest form of action, in my opinion, is the action you take within yourself. Crossing your internal bridges.

Several years back I consulted with the CEO of a very successful company. At least, it was perceived as a successful company, though internally it had 'lost its way'. Business was still going well, but the employees weren't happy and the atmosphere was negative. It was only a matter of time until its revenue and profit would decline too, just like the workplace culture of the once happier staff. These situations, where there is a big gap between the way things look on the outside and how they really are, always make me curious. I can tell you, I wasn't surprised to discover that the same could be said for the CEO herself, Christine; she came across as polished and successful, yet inside she felt as if she had lost her way. She used the word 'false' to describe how she felt.

'I'm leaving,' she announced during our session. 'I'm going to be brave and step away. It's not working, I'm failing. I'll do the right thing and let someone else lead the company.'

Deciding to leave a workplace is a major decision. Christine was deeply invested in the company, she loved it. And although her decision to leave might at first seem like stepping across a 'narrow bridge', I had a feeling that the bridge she truly needed to cross was actually within herself.

'I feel for you, Christine,' I told her. 'I know how much you care and how frustrating it must be not to be able to change things the way you'd like to. But I'd like to ask you something, and please take a moment to reflect. When you think about leaving, are you moving towards something or running away from something?'

'Away, of course,' she replied. 'Away from not being able to fix this problem. Away from not doing the CEO job well enough. Away from disappointing everyone.'

It was obvious that these feelings were taking their toll on her. I had another question: 'Are you giving up your role as CEO to run from a situation you genuinely don't believe you can change... or are you running away from something inside you, from yourself?'

Christine took a moment and then smiled sadly. 'Well,' she said, 'I think we both know the answer to that question.'

There is a big difference between crossing a bridge to get *away* from something and crossing a bridge *towards* something. Yes, sometimes we do need to run away, to escape a person or situation that isn't good for us. But often, when we choose to run it's because we don't believe in ourselves – because we've lost faith or confidence in our ability to make things better. It's difficult to keep trying when we'd really like to move on and forget, but the truth is that we won't forget or change that easily, and if we run away, we may still find ourselves facing that same bridge, again, elsewhere.

I asked Christine if she thought there was a way to turn the situation around. Could she look at this as an opportunity to try one more time, to change something inside herself, and cross that narrow bridge of fear of failure?

'I'll stay,' she said, 'and come out stronger on the other side.' And so she did. With great success!

Christine faced her fears and took action. She dared to 'fail harder' both for herself and for the company. She was bolder, more creative and more innovative in the ideas she implemented after this decision. This doesn't mean she was looking to fail, but rather that she allowed herself to potentially 'fail harder'. Knowing you might fail allows you to bring your authentic, brilliant self to the world, to your relationships, to your workplace. It means pursuing your purpose and aspirations fully and wholeheartedly. Doing your best. Not being afraid.

Children can learn this, too. A few days ago, my seven-year-old son came home from his first day back at school. With great excitement and enthusiasm, he told me, '*Ima*, my teacher hung up a poster at school today and it says, "*Maycinng meestakes is prooff that you're trying.*" So now it's okay to make mistakes at school!'

It made my heart sing. It's good for him to learn that setbacks and disappointments are part of life. That it's okay. That making mistakes is part of his journey. This lesson will help him and his friends become more resilient, more agile, stronger.

During our lives, we come to many bridges. Some rise above a great abyss, and crossing them truly requires courage. But there are many smaller bridges that we don't always recognise as such. Signing up for a course you always wanted to take but weren't sure you'd get accepted to, or picking up dance classes again although you haven't danced in years are both bridges you could cross. So too, is applying for a job although there are hundreds of other candidates, or adopting a pet, because, yes, you believe in your ability to take care of another living thing. As you look to better your life, don't just look out for the big, heavy, iconic bridges to cross. Look for small bridges, beautiful bridges that were built with care, bridges that blend in with the scenery, all the little bridges that make up your life. When you see these bridges and cross them, you'll be living a life of 'doing', where action replaces fear.

Of course, some bridges are narrower than others. Either way, the first step is the hardest. Often we don't embark upon a 'narrow bridge' journey because we replay in our head our past mistakes and are consumed by doubts. It's at these moments of self-doubt that I try to remember that time my life coach asked if I would want to get rid of the 'anxiety part' of me, and how I so definitively thought, 'no!' My anxieties are part of me. My failures are part of me. I am stronger now and I needed them to get here.

My best way out of fear is taking some kind of action. Moving forward. Once I realised this, I decided to stop living in constant fear of failure, disappointment and death, and I started choosing life. It's a far better lifestyle.

A Very Narrow Bridge

This phrase, 'a very narrow bridge', is taken from a well-known song based on the words of Rebbe Nachman of Breslov. The narrow bridge represents the scary, unknown path ahead of you in your life. The rest of the song encourages you to 'have no fear at all'. We must try to take that first step onto our narrow bridge, whatever it may be. We must always move forwards if we want to conquer our fears. Just the action of taking a single step may be enough to change things for you.

IF YOU CHANGE NOTHING, NOTHING WILL CHANGE

Now, over to you. I invite you to think how you could replace fear with action and cross your internal and external life bridges. Remember, crossing a 'bridge', big or small, is taking action. It is believing in yourself. It is allowing yourself to potentially fail in order to grow stronger. Answer one or two questions, or all of them, in order to deepen your learning about yourself.

1 Reflect on a time when you took a leap of faith. What happened? What did you learn about yourself and others that helped you grow?

2 What is your most recent 'fail harder' experience? What were your learnings? How did you grow out of the failure?

3 What narrow bridge (big or small) do you have in front of you right now? Where are you with making a decision about if and how to cross that bridge?

4 How are you feeling about crossing that bridge? Who could help you cross it?

5 Which current fear or concern could you replace with positive action? What could that positive action be?

5
GROW YOUR BROKEN HEART

'In every sadness there is benefit.'
Proverbs 14:23

At the age of twenty-three I fell in love. He was all the things that weren't me at the time – fearless, fun, confident and living in the moment. He drove a sporty motorbike, did all the things he wanted to, lived life on the edge and fully trusted his instincts. He had a large group of friends from the same elite unit in the military and they were close, like brothers, always looking out for each other. I allowed myself to cross the bridge of falling in love – totally, with all my heart. I chose to be completely open and authentic with him, sharing my life experiences, my fears, everything. I was like an open book. I was 'all in' in our relationship, and I thought he was the same. In fact, I was convinced that he was *the one*.

One beautiful Tel Aviv day we went for a stroll on the beach. He said he wanted to talk. I suddenly had butterflies in my stomach – was he about to ask me to marry him? This was the moment I had longed for my whole life – to find the man who would love me as I loved him, who would want to spend the rest of his life with me, who would cherish me and understand me, accept me for exactly who I am.

As I turned to him, expecting to hear *the* question, I saw tears in his eyes. But something felt wrong. They weren't the kind of tears I was expecting.

'I'm sorry, Michal,' he said. 'It's over.'

Over?? I was in utter shock. 'Why?'

'I'm sorry,' he said again. 'I love you but... when I think to myself, "Who would I take with me to a deserted island? Who can't I possibly live without?" I realise *it isn't you*. You're not my future wife. I can't see this going anywhere beyond what it already is, so it's better to end it now. I love you. You're just not the one.'

I felt like I was living a nightmare. I could almost hear a voice in the back of my head shouting, 'wake up, wake up,' but I couldn't wake up. It was very real. I was awake, and he was leaving me. Everything I'd thought about my future was gone. I'd bared my soul to him, had the courage to be myself, and it wasn't enough. As he looked at me with pity, I felt like I was about to faint. The sun was still shining, the surfers were still catching waves, the world had not stopped moving, but I felt the most surreal sensation. It was like my heart had paused, and I wondered if it would ever beat again, now that it was shattered into a million tiny pieces.

This might sound dramatic, but for me – totally in love, for once totally safe and honest in my relationship – it was horrible pain. In his army service, this man that was now breaking my heart had been a bomb disposal expert. I remember thinking that he was doing just the opposite to me: he had set a bomb himself, stood back and watched it explode. I felt like my heart would never – *could never* – be mended.

My recovery was slow. I lost a quarter of my body weight, along with any interest in going out, enjoying life or meeting someone new. I lost faith in loving again. The only thing I hoped for was to stop hurting so much. He was the first thing I thought about when I woke up, and my last thought before falling asleep. I wished I could wipe his memory out of my system, forget I'd ever met him. But that wasn't possible. Everything reminded me of him – every motorbike I heard, every food I knew he loved, each time I heard 'our' songs. I felt like I would be broken forever. 'Nothing and nobody will ever repair my heart,' I told my younger sister, who was desperately trying to help.

I had been raised for perfection, and failure was one of my greatest fears. Now that this man had left me I was not only heartbroken, but my ego was badly bruised, too. I lost my self-confidence and thought of myself as a complete failure. And because failure was the worst thing I could think of, the sense of brokenness was even more painful.

It took over two years to start healing. Gradually, I found my heart getting stronger. When it came, my healing was from a place of acceptance: I realised that I couldn't be everyone's chosen companion on a desert island. And he was right – we clearly weren't right for each other. But could I ever love again? How could I mend my heart and make it ready for someone else?

Brokenness

Long after my heartbreak, I discovered a life-changing principle that offers a new perspective on brokenness. It's a totally different outlook to the one I had previously and it goes against how our society usually views suffering. It changed how I felt about 'breaking'. And it changed my ideas about love and perfection as well. I'd like to share it with you, because I believe it'll help you, too:

> *There is nothing more complete than a broken heart.*
> Rabbi Menachem Mendel Morgenstern, the Kotzker Rebbe

Take a moment. Read it again.

Meditate on the meaning: There is nothing more complete – more whole, more full – than your broken heart. In other words, your heart is more complete now that it's broken than it was before.

How can that be?

Here is the explanation (which I love!). When a heart breaks, it breaks into pieces with cracks in between. This saying suggests that true growth takes place in the cracks, between the broken shards. It's in the space between that your wisdom, maturity and strength can grow into beautiful imperfection.

I find it interesting that Jewish wisdom and Japanese philosophy seem to have arrived at the same approach towards brokenness. *Kitsungi*, the Japanese art of ceramics repair, which literally means 'to join with gold', is an expression of ancient Zen philosophy, according to which, there shouldn't be any attempt to hide brokenness, but rather, to piece the broken pieces together again and to understand that that's where growth takes place: in the cracks. Something broken, when put back together again, can be more beautiful than ever before.

No one wants to have their heart broken. No one wants to discover they were wrong about being loved, to lose confidence or feel like a failure. But the growth that comes from these feelings of worthlessness and pain can ultimately be greater than the pain itself. For me, the lesson was that, despite the risk of rejection, falling in love was still a narrow bridge worth crossing.

I also learnt that I didn't need to spend all that time trying to mend my broken heart. I was never supposed to *mend* my brokenness, to try to get back to what I was before. Not only is that impossible, but now my brokenness is a part of me. It makes me more complete.

Looking back, it's obvious that if I hadn't suffered that agonising breakup, if that boyfriend hadn't left me, I would never have met my husband Yair – my *one*. But more than that, I wouldn't have become who I am – *the complete and broken version of me*.

Your Soul Never Breaks

As painful as my heartbreak was, deep inside I knew that I would eventually move on and that 'this too shall pass'. Heartbreak is painful, as is a sense of loss, ongoing emptiness and feeling you are not in control of a situation. But know this: your soul stays intact. The soul doesn't break. The soul is here for a reason and once the heart adjusts again, life will continue forward, always seeking to fulfil the soul's purpose. We are stronger than we think. We can trust the soul, even when the heart cannot be relied on.

But what about those heartaches that feel simply impossible to survive?

By now you know that the psychiatrist and neurologist Viktor Frankl is an inspiration to me, and that his desire to find purpose even in the most terrible of situations has helped me, and others, understand our meaning in life.

In his book *Man's Search for Meaning*, Frankl talks about his time in the Auschwitz concentration camp. He describes how he and hundreds of others were put through physical and mental torture and came close to death. But during this time, he also observed a pattern that fascinated him: the prisoners who showed more of a

will to survive were the ones who had found meaning in
their lives.

Frankl shared the meaning in his life that kept *him*
from giving up: it was his love for his wife Tilly and the
hope that he would find her after the war. Even though
Frankl accepted the possibility that she might not
survive, it was his hope and love for her that kept him
alive through the most intolerable circumstances.

After the war, Frankl searched for Tilly. However, he
soon learnt that his beloved wife had died of typhus in
the concentration camp Bergen-Belsen. He wrote a letter
to friends in September 1945, describing his sadness and
loneliness since learning of her death. He says, 'I have
nothing more to hope for and nothing more to fear... I
live out of conscience.'

Frankl continues by saying he has started to focus on
his work, re-dictating his manuscript with a view to
having it published, and to help with his rehabilitation:

> But no success can make me happy, everything is
> weightless, void, vain in my eyes, I feel distant from
> everything. It all says nothing to me, means nothing.
> The best have not returned ...

Yet, despite his grief, Frankl is able to look back on his
experiences in the death camps, and his observations that
even in the depths of despair, meaning can lead to hope:

> But I now see things in a larger dimension. I see
> increasingly that life is so very meaningful, that in
> suffering and even in failure there must still be meaning.
> And my only consolation lies in the fact that I can say in

all good conscience that I realized the opportunities that presented themselves to me, I mean to say: that I turned them into reality. This is the case with respect to my short marriage to Tilly. What we have experienced cannot be undone, it has been, but this having-been is perhaps the most certain form of being.

Excerpt from letter reproduced in *Man's Search for Meaning* by Viktor E. Frankl, (Beacon Press, 2014)

The love Frankl had for his wife and the hope that she was still alive were what had given him meaning in Auschwitz. Now, when he was finally a free man, she was gone. It is clear from his letter that Frankl reached a dangerous place within himself. But he also knew the importance of having a purpose in life – he had experienced the power of it himself.

Frankl's ideas about this can be summed up as a mathematical equation:

$$D = S - M$$

Despair equals suffering without meaning.

Frankl took his own advice. He found internal strength and resilience, not despite his grief, but *because of it*. Just as life and the world had changed, he knew that so should he. He found a new purpose: he made it his mission to tell the world about his time in Auschwitz and the psychological discoveries he had made there. He knew that, whatever his current circumstances, he had a purpose to fulfil here on Earth. He knew he had to share his discoveries with the medical, psychiatric and wider world. Having that purpose meant that there was less room for fear, depression and emptiness in his life. He decided to move forward rather than stay still and grieve to the exclusion of everything else. He decided to do something. His book *Man's Search for Meaning* has sold more than nine million copies, has been reprinted dozens of times and has been translated into at least twenty-four languages. He was right – finding this new purpose, even after losing his soulmate, was what the world needed him to do.

Breaking Ourselves

Life can sometimes put us through great suffering. But there is another kind of brokenness – one that we bring on ourselves – the brokenness that comes from our own thoughts or actions. The disappointment we feel about our own actions can leave us broken inside, too. For example, when we hurt someone badly or break someone else's heart, when we make a very bad judgement call or display truly negative behaviour.

When I coach leaders on developing their leadership, I make sure that I 'see' the whole person, not just their professional persona. As they open up, quite a few of them choose to reveal great amounts of regret, shame or guilt. Some of them are living with never-ending sadness as a result of the painful struggles that go on inside them, of events from the past or of flaws they see daily in their character. So often, I've found that leaders are secretly feeling hopelessness and despair.

Guilt, shame and regret result in a sense of brokenness. They are very different emotions, but they all lead to us feeling as if we are in pieces. There are two ways we can react to feeling this kind of brokenness: we can let it consume everything or we can understand that this, too, is an opportunity for growth. We don't have to remove those feelings, we can grow *from* them.

As I'm writing this chapter we have just finished celebrating Yom Kippur, the Day of Atonement. It is the holiest day of the Jewish year. The spiritual preparations for Yom Kippur, which is also a day of fasting, start more than a month in advance. A big part of the preparation is internal, a reflective journey during which we think about our actions over the past year.

The year I first reconnected with my Jewish faith, I dug deep into my soul during those weeks of preparation before Yom Kippur. I followed the brilliant 60 *Days: A Spiritual Guide to the High Holidays*, a book written by Simon Jacobson, that includes daily practices and reflections. I asked my friends and family for forgiveness for any hurtful things I had said or done to them that year, and I planned to arrive at the holiest of days ready to become the best version of myself. I even travelled to Israel with my family, wanting to experience this special holy day with my parents and sister, in my childhood synagogue.

When Yom Kippur arrived, I headed to synagogue with my husband and parents and embarked on twenty-five hours of fasting, praying and focusing on internal commitment for change. But as I entered the prayer hall and positioned myself on my chair, ready to dive into my prayers, my eyes landed on a woman I knew. She was an old friend from high school, always popular, always top of the class – someone who had long been my 'idol'. Over the years, I'd continued to hear about her talents, successes and achievements. She remained a woman who represented 'perfection' to me, a woman to admire and also, if I am honest, a woman to envy.

Although I was supposed to be praying, I found myself secretly watching her. My eyes followed her movements. I strained to overhear the conversations she quietly had with a few women. I observed how she gracefully waved to her husband who sat a few rows away from her. I scanned her clothes, her body. I watched how she held herself, how she acted. When one of her children approached her, asking a million questions, she replied patiently and calmed him down in no time. She seemed to hold herself in an effortless way, looking so comfortable in her own skin, sure and confident in every move. She was pretty, too, in an effortless manner. She had it all.

Then I caught myself.

What am I doing? I thought. This day is about asking for forgiveness from my family, my friends and God and starting afresh, trying to become a kinder, better version of myself, and here I am feeling jealous of this woman who I have hardly spoken to in years. What is wrong with me? Why do I even care? Why am I obsessively thinking about her? Now? On today of all days?

I hated myself for having these thoughts but the more I wanted to be rid of them, the more I obsessed over them. I assumed they stemmed from my own insecurities, from my own negative thoughts about myself, from my fear of not being *enough*. It frustrated me that I couldn't just be happy with my lot. Why did I still have these destructive thoughts? Why did I have to always crave more?

I was very miserable on that Yom Kippur. I felt like

such a failure. I was actively trying to grow as a person and there I was, thinking petty, jealous thoughts – on Yom Kippur of all days! I now know that I was being too hard on myself and that these types of thoughts are common, particularly at solemn moments. In fact, I have since learnt that the Baal Shem Tov himself talked about this phenomenon of 'strange thoughts' that surface when you are trying to concentrate.

Do you know that feeling when, during prayer or meditation, or when you are trying to fall asleep, just as you find quiet and inner peace, some of the most negative and disruptive thoughts bubble up uninvited? Well, there is a reason why this happens, and it gives us an insight into how the soul works.

The reason these thoughts arise is because the soul wants to help us self-correct. It wants us to repair our negative thoughts, so it brings them to the surface at quiet, reflective moments when we are sure to notice them. The Baal Shem Tov taught that these negative thoughts should not make us feel ashamed or embarrassed, but rather should be looked upon as an opportunity for self-observation and self-correction. Our soul is showing us exactly what we need to work on.

The jealousy I felt is an example of internal brokenness, of those 'strange thoughts'. When I acknowledged these thoughts on Yom Kippur, I felt broken, imperfect. But when I later encountered the saying, 'There is nothing more complete than a broken heart,' I immediately sensed its deep wisdom. My soul wanted me to see where I was broken so I could fix it. There is endless potential for growth everywhere. Even the broken shards, even the most uncomfortable thoughts, even the brokenness of my own imperfection can eventually be transformed into something good.

This take on imperfection is a central theme of Jewish wisdom. Imperfection is welcomed, even valued, as a positive tool for growth. In Jewish thought, the two opposing forces inside us are known as the *yetzer tov*, the good inclination, and the *yetzer hara*, the bad inclination. The perpetual conflict between the good inclination, as it encourages us to be kind and thoughtful, and the bad inclination, urging us to be selfish or to hurt other people, can make us feel like we are broken inside. But actually, the struggle is what we are designed for: to learn, to self-correct, to grow. What feels like brokenness is what makes us human.

When we feel the bad inclination, we need to know that this is not our only voice. Yes, there are two opposing forces inside us but the choice is always ours – how we think, speak and act – and that is what makes all the difference.

Acknowledging my jealousy on that Yom Kippur was an important journey of growth for me. Without that initial struggle, how would I have learnt? Embracing those times when the bad inclination got the better of the good inclination not only allowed me to accept myself, it allowed me to grow. When we look at our struggling, conflicted inclinations – really honestly and truthfully – we put ourselves in the best position to grow. The key is to never stop believing that we can improve.

The Value of Broken Things

I used to avoid brokenness. I used to get rid of broken things. If something broke in the house – a toaster, an alarm clock, or if a blanket had a tear in it – I would get rid of it and buy a new one. If I got my nails done and one of them chipped, I would remove the varnish and paint it again – back to perfection.

I did the same with my emotional scars, with the brokenness inside me. I was trying to 'fix' what had gone wrong in me, hide the scars, make myself 'perfect'. That is, until I learnt the value of broken things. Today I keep that chipped nail as a reminder and I won't get rid of the torn blanket. I'll sew it up myself. And the broken toaster? I use things like that as a door stop or a toy. Yes, really.

When Moses received the Ten Commandments from God on Mount Sinai, he spent forty days and forty nights on the mountain. The Israelites grew impatient after they miscalculated the day of his return. 'Where is he? What are we waiting for?' they asked each other. This ultimately resulted in the Israelites building a forbidden idol, a golden calf. When Moses finally came down, holding the set of tablets with the Ten Commandments engraved on them, he saw the idol and threw the tablets to the ground where they shattered. After reprimanding and punishing the sinners, Moses went back up the mountain and begged God to forgive the Israelites for their grave sin. He pleaded for them and eventually, on Yom Kippur, God agreed, granting His forgiveness. A new, second set of tablets was carved and handed to Moses by God. It was an opportunity to start again.

There are many lessons to be learnt from this dramatic

story. But what I love most is that the original tablets, now broken into pieces, were not thrown away. In fact, they were kept alongside the new, unbroken, tablets in the holiest of places – the Ark of the Covenant in the Holy of Holies. The broken pieces were revered and honoured because they symbolised and commemorated our mistakes, as well as our capacity to gain forgiveness. Why keep something so broken in the holiest of places? Why keep a reminder of past transgression and pain? Because brokenness and wholeness sit side by side. Indeed, wholeness is born and built out of brokenness.

Where would we be without forgiveness? Without hope? Who would we be if we were never to fail, never allowed a second chance? If we didn't forgive, we would lack the capacity to learn from mistakes, to repair and move forward. We would resent others and ourselves. We would hold on to anger for far too long.

If you've ever been to a Jewish wedding or heard what they're like, you'll know that they can be a very big affair! There's food, music and dancing, and often hundreds of family members, friends, neighbours and colleagues who come to celebrate with the couple. The ceremony takes place under a *chuppah* (traditional Jewish wedding canopy) where the couple commit to their sacred union. At the end of the ceremony the groom does something unique – a Jewish tradition that goes back hundreds of years – he breaks a glass by stomping on it! Why? Why smash a glass on your wedding day? There are several different explanations of this tradition, but here is my favourite one: the groom breaks a glass as a reminder that things will always break, even in the happiest of marriages. And those hard moments can and should be used to develop a stronger marriage. The couple must learn to accept brokenness and use it as a vehicle for growth, to become even more whole.

Get Comfortable with the Uncomfortable

Throughout your life, your heart will get broken in multiple, different ways – by breakups, rejection, guilt, failure, loss and shame. One heartbreak doesn't protect you from future breaks, one shattering doesn't prevent future pain. We are designed to break, but we are also designed to live life to its fullest even when we are broken.

When we get comfortable with feeling uncomfortable and accept that life was never supposed to be perfect, we allow ourselves to look at life as an opportunity to better ourselves. It's a chance to learn how to deal with setbacks, to make space to feel the pain and then, always, keep on going forward. Perhaps we need to force ourselves to take those first steps forward until it becomes easier, but yes, life is our lifelong chance to grow.

If I think of the moments I've been most proud of myself, it's those times when I had to overcome difficulties, and I survived. And not only that, I bounced back stronger. I think that's why, when that life coach once asked me if, given the chance, I would erase all my pain and suffering, and 'cut out' that part from who I am, my answer was 'no'. Even though I hadn't, at that time, started to explore Jewish wisdom, something inside me simply knew that even the fear and anxiety makes me who I am. I sometimes wonder what would happen if all of us, as individuals and as a society, could start viewing brokenness not as something negative but as an opportunity for growth.

Jewish wisdom teaches:

Weeping is lodged in one side of my heart, and joy is lodged in the other.
Zohar III 75a

We cannot be happy all the time. But just like with the broken and unbroken tablets, it is possible to carry sadness and joy, failure and forgiveness, heartbreak and hope, fear and purpose, all together inside us.

Brokenness

*Feeling broken is universal: everyone feels broken in some way at some point in their lives. Brokenness is not something to be feared; it doesn't need to be fixed. Broken people should not be discarded. In fact, it is in the space between the shards of our broken hearts and our fragmented selves where we will learn and grow. The cracks are what make us **us**. They make us unique. The cracks make us more beautiful, more special, more powerful and more whole.*

IF YOU CHANGE NOTHING, NOTHING WILL CHANGE

No one wants their heart to break and yet it has most probably happened to you at some point in your life. This chapter invites you to look at brokenness from a new perspective – from the inspirational notion that, 'Nothing is more complete than a broken heart.' You don't have to revisit hard times or remind yourself of the pain, but rather, I'd like to invite you to focus on the growth and learnings you have taken from those moments. Feel free to answer one, two or all the coaching questions here with a positive, growth mindset

1 What has been your most meaningful experience of 'breaking' or 'brokenness'? What did you learn from that experience about yourself and your internal strength, and about your 'completeness'?

2 If you choose to see the space between the broken pieces of you as a place for growth, what could that look like? What could you fill the cracks with?

3 If you allowed yourself to let go of perfection – in both your views of yourself and the world – who or what could you grow to become?

4 What do you need to let go of (a memory, an experience, a regret, a mistake) in order to move forward with your life?

5 What are you most proud of in your life? What have been the most meaningful moments and events, when you have felt growth?

6
MAKE SPACE FOR OTHERS

'Distancing is for the purpose of drawing near.'

Rebbe Nachman of Breslov

When I married my husband, Yair, I thought I knew what a good marriage should look like. I didn't expect a fairy tale version of marriage – after all, I wasn't a child. I expected a version of my parents' marriage: a solid, respectful and long-term marriage, with a mutual commitment that puts family first. 'Let's have a great, strong marriage,' is what I said to Yair, but what I actually meant was that I wanted *their* marriage. There was no space in my mind to consider any way of being married other than like my parents.

And so, I entered married life assuming that I had all the answers to how our relationship should be. Every time there was conflict or tension between us, I expected Yair to behave the way he 'should' based on the model I had in my mind. And if he didn't react or behave as 'expected', I found myself disappointed, hurt or angry. 'Stop comparing us to your parents,' he would say. 'You can't assume that just because your parents have a good marriage, you know it all. You don't and we are not them.'

He was right. After years of trying to impose my vision of marriage onto him, onto us and – in many ways – onto myself, I realised that I hadn't left any room for myself and Yair as a couple to establish *our marriage*. I hadn't made space for us to establish *our way*. We needed our own methods for dealing with conflict, for solving problems, for navigating life together. I hadn't made space for my husband because I thought I knew it all. I hadn't left anything for us to work out *together*.

This reminds me of a CEO I consulted with many years ago. He was extremely influential within his industry, always switched on, but not a great listener. It seemed like he had everything he wanted – a glittering career, power, money, a family – and yet he was far from being happy and fulfilled. Throughout our meetings he shared his frustration at not feeling respected enough. He would share stories of his board of directors and fellow senior leaders failing to appreciate his seniority. He felt the same about his children, and even his wife.

One day he asked me, 'Why does no one really respect me? I guide them, offer solutions, give lots of advice and ideas; I bring them my experience and my knowledge, and yet I still feel that they don't value me – it's like they are stepping all over me.'

'It's an interesting question,' I said. 'Do you have any idea why?'

'No,' he said. 'I do all the right things, but they still don't respect me.'

'I have a theory,' I said. 'But it might make you feel uncomfortable. Shall I tell you?'

'Yes,' he replied, 'Tell me, I really want to know what I'm doing to deserve such disrespect.'

'I wonder whether it feels as if people are stepping on your pride,' I said, 'because you are taking up too much of *their* space. Is there any space free of your pride?'

Taking up too much space – existential space, not physical space – from those around us is something many of us do unintentionally. We might think we are being helpful, but when we impose too much of ourselves – whether by talking over someone, offering too many ideas and solutions or not listening humbly to how others feel or think – we are taking up too much space. We're assuming our way is the best without listening to alternatives. But why do we always feel the need to shout the loudest, to solve all the problems, to make it all about *us*?

Because of fear. We are so attached to our ego, so afraid that something will harm us, that we consider our own survival above anyone else's. We want to assert our knowledge, show our experience in any given situation. We don't want to appear ignorant or uninformed. Maybe we take over the conversation as a way to control its outcome. Perhaps we choose to hear what we want to hear, rather than listen with curiosity and empathy, because we fear we won't approve of the other opinion. We fall in love with our own ideas, we think we know what's right. And so we don't leave space for others.

Taking up too much space doesn't necessarily mean being loud or intrusive. It just means we're trying to dominate through our presence – and that we might not be leaving enough room for others to grow, shine, make mistakes or, sometimes, just speak. This way of being doesn't allow for diversity of opinions and voices. It seriously limits how far a conversation can go and how much a family or a team can progress, learn or grow. As I said, this was something I struggled with in the early days of my married life.

That is, until I learnt about the principle of *tzimtzum*. In more ways than one, learning about *tzimtzum* has changed my life.

I was initially hesitant as to whether I should include the mystical concept of *tzimtzum* in this book because it is so deep, complex and, more than anything, holy. After much consideration I decided to share it with you because I truly believe it can be life changing. I will talk about it in my layman's terms, and I ask that you appreciate its holiness, deep meaning and importance. Please treat it with the utmost respect, intrigue and care.

Tzimtzum

In Hebrew, the word *tzimtzum* means 'contraction' or 'concealment'. The concept of *tzimtzum* was established by the sixteenth-century mystic, Rabbi Isaac Luria, known as the Arizal, and documented by his dedicated disciple, Rabbi Chaim Vital, in the classic Kabbalistic text, *Etz Chaim*.

In order to understand *tzimtzum*, we have to start from the very beginning. What was there before the world was created? According to the Torah, there was nothing: no existence, no time and space – and certainly no human beings, animals, land, oceans, plants, sky, earth, sun or darkness: nothing of the world as we know it today. There was only God and His infinite light, which, in Jewish mysticism, is referred to as *Ohr Ein Sof*.

Prior to Creation, there was only the infinite Ohr Ein Sof filling all existence. When it arose in G d's Will to create worlds and emanate the emanated... He contracted (in Hebrew 'tzimtzum') Himself in the point at the centre, in the very centre of His light. He restricted that light, distancing it to the sides surrounding the central point, so that there remained a void, a hollow empty space, away from the central point... After this tzimtzum... He drew down from the Ohr Ein Sof a single straight line [of light] from His light surrounding [the void] from above to below [into the void], and it chained down descending into that void... In the space of that void He emanated, created, formed and made all the worlds.

Etz Chaim heichal A"K, anaf 2

You can spend a lifetime studying the concept of *tzimtzum*, and this fascinating explanation from *Etz Chaim* is not easy to grasp. Let's take it step by step.

Before the creation of the world as we know it, everything was filled with what is known as *Ohr Ein Sof*. Literally, this Hebrew phrase means 'light without end' or 'infinite light'. Before anything else existed, there was God, filling everything with His infinite light, leaving no vacant space. There was no beginning, no end, no boundaries or limitations, only one singular, seamless light – everywhere, everything – filled with the capacity to create.

If God fills everything and is Himself everything, if all space is filled with the *Ohr Ein Sof*, how could He create something new? There is no room for anyone or anything else. Where would human beings go? And animals, plants, oceans and rocks? Where would the sun fit? And the moon?

God wanted to make room for all these things, so He *contracted* part of His light to make space.

How is that possible? Try to imagine it. Although the *Ohr Ein Sof* was everywhere and everything, God wanted to make space for His creations. That's why He decided to contract the infiniteness of His presence and make space for something else: us. That is *tzimtzum* – the practice of contracting yourself to let something else grow in the newly empty space. When God did this, a world was born.

Tzimtzum is such an inspiring idea and it offers us an opportunity to shift the way we think about our presence. It teaches us the power of restraint, and it helps us discover the potential of giving others the space they need. *Tzimtzum* shows us that, if we learn how to take up less space for ourselves and make more space for others, our sense of fulfilment, joy and meaning doesn't diminish – it increases.

Writing about this reminded me of a time in my childhood when my mother made space for me. As I've already mentioned, I was a fearful child. Nightmares were a regular occurrence. Almost every night, I'd walk across the corridor to my parents' bedroom, where the door was always open. I never made a noise or tried to wake them up, I just stood there, in front of their bedroom door, and looked at my mother sleeping peacefully. I knew from experience – from the previous night and from the many, many nights before – that, although she was sleeping, she would always, and I mean *always*, sense that I was there and open her eyes. She would look straight into my eyes and, without uttering a word, shuffle closer to my father's side of the bed to make space for me. As I crawled in next to her, still shaken from the nightmares, I knew that I had nothing to worry about. I would simply fall asleep. No words needed to be said, and we would never speak of it the next morning. She just made space for my fear and, in doing so, she made it go away.

I kept waking up and going into my mother's side of the bed until the age of ten or eleven. And I eventually stopped – not because she told me I was too old for this, or because she took me to therapy to get over it. I stopped when I began to feel her strength and confidence while still in my own bed. And I knew there was always space for me next to her if I needed it.

Presence Through Absence

So how do you practise *tzimtzum*? Applying it to everyday life has taught me the secret of a meaningful marriage, effective parenting and nurturing leadership. It showed me how I could become a better version of myself, it helped me tame my ego, which I've always struggled with, and it inspired me to make a conscious shift in my mindset. Practising *tzimtzum* made me happier, more content and, ironically, more confident. And if you ask the people around me – it makes them happier too.

Being present with your child, life partner, friend, colleague or neighbour doesn't mean that you have to take up all the space you can. You don't have to make your presence obvious or dominant. There is another way of bringing ourselves into important relationships: we can actively and deliberately choose to take up less space, to contract ourselves at certain times and make space for others by limiting something of ourselves, our influence, our control. This *does not* mean that we will undermine ourselves, that we will 'lose' any of ourselves. On the contrary, when we surrender the need to show the world how much space we take up, it is a sign that we actually feel more complete and comfortable with who we are. And the more we feel comfortable in our own skin, the less space we will need to take.

We live in an evidence-based world, where we are asked to show and prove things. If we can't prove it – it's not true. That's what I have been told most of my life, but I challenge that doctrine with the idea of *tzimtzum*. Just because you can't see something doesn't mean it's not there. Concealing can be just as impactful as revealing, if not more so.

This concept applies to all aspects of life. For instance, in order to be an inspirational leader or parent, you don't need to display all your experience, wisdom and knowledge in front of everyone. Instead, you should consider your audience and what they need from you and your leadership. Adjust yourself to meet their expectations and needs, even if it means giving less advice, guidance or direction than you are capable of. We should always consider how much of ourselves to 'present' for the other party to feel comfortable, and to allow them space to grow.

As I write this, one of my children is going through a challenging time at school. They are unsure of what to do and feeling vulnerable. How should I respond? Should I share all that *I've* learnt about people in my life, the hurtful, painful experiences I've had, all the things that have gone wrong for me in my friendships and relationships over the years? Would that be helpful? Would that serve their needs right now? Would they even have the capacity to understand? The answer to all these questions is no. By sharing my own experiences and telling them more than their capacity or need to understand, I would be focusing on me and not on *them*. I wouldn't be meeting my child where they are at right now.

So what can I do instead of solving their issues for them or giving *my* answers?

I should practise *tzimtzum*. I must actively resist taking up too much, or all the space. I need to contract some of my experience, to share just what they need to know and just what they are able to understand right now. This approach isn't patronising, it's sensitive. It's focusing on the other person. Think of it this way: although I share less than my full knowledge and experience, it's not *less* useful for my child – it's *more* useful. I am adding value by contracting what I share.

In all the years I went to therapy, I was never really given space in this way. It would have been helpful to me if some of my therapists had been familiar with Professor Mordechai Rotenberg, a world-leading expert in psychology, who has written many books on the usefulness of *tzimtzum* in the therapy process. Professor Rotenberg promotes a school of thought in which the therapist truly makes space for their client's full self, without judgement. At the heart of this approach is *tzimtzum*. The therapist gives the patient space to express their own interpretations.

As a therapist, a friend, a leader or a parent, making space is an act of kindness, of empowerment. It assumes that there is no conflict between you and the other person but rather the potential for two or more people to light up the world side by side, in harmony.

Leaders and companies often think differently. They look at work – and life – as a series of mini battles that they always have to 'win'. Whether that's winning a project, getting recognition or gaining the upper hand in a friendship or relationship, people often feel that they have to take up space, to impress, to show their power, to secure their position. They assume the spotlight should be on them, and less on others. And it's not only leaders. Our natural tendency is to assume that holding back some of our power, making space for others, will risk our position or influence. But the opposite is true. When we make space for others, when we shine the spotlight on them, we create an atmosphere of goodwill and commitment in the long run.

Everyone Needs Space

Let's go back to the tension I had early on in my marriage, when I took all the space by assuming I knew what our life together should look like. Like most couples, we had each arrived at the relationship with our own beliefs on what a good marriage should look like. We each wanted our relationship to work, but we had different ideas on how to get there. Each of us carried our own parents' marriage in our minds – that was our individual benchmark, for better or for worse. We entered our shared life together as two individuals, both frightened to let go of any part of ourselves. Neither of us considered making any real adjustment to ourselves in relation to the other.

Here's an example. When we were still dating, in the early 2000s, whenever I'd call Yair on his mobile, or he'd call me, one of the first questions I'd ask him was 'Where are you'? I'm afraid I did not mean the question in the philosophical or psychological sense of 'where are you in your journey of life?' as we discussed in chapter two. I just wanted to know where he physically was. You might assume I was possessive, anxious or was afraid of being abandoned again, but whatever the reason, that's what I asked. And it drove him crazy. 'Why do you keep asking me where I am? Why does it matter?' he'd ask irritably, and I, in turn, became defensive: 'Why are you making such a big deal out of it? Just tell me where you are!' He would refuse to tell me. And this was an ongoing source of tension until I realised that by asking this question, I was putting him off from wanting to call me. It made him feel as if I didn't trust or respect him, and most importantly, that I wasn't giving him space. Once I realised this, I stopped asking him. And you know what? Once I gave him that space, he started sharing his plans and whereabouts naturally. We were both happier.

Today, after nearly twenty years together, we have adapted and learnt to co-exist. We did this by learning how to practise *tzimtzum*. Instead of competing with one another, we slowly tried to find a way to make more space for each other and to 'contract' ourselves for the other when needed. In doing so we created a void of potential, a vacant space in which to build our own 'togetherness'.

Giving space gives back more than I ever imagined. Don't think though, that it's been easy. Practising *tzimtzum* requires flexibility, self-awareness and honesty. And it's work in progress, just like life itself. An ongoing process of acknowledging others and truly seeing them and caring for them. It requires empathy, not ego.

Practising *tzimtzum* has improved every relationship in my life and I've seen it improve situations in the workplace, too, including ongoing conflict, tension and 'ego games'. Making space is highly effective if you are a manager or team leader, or if you simply have a passion to help people grow. I can't say this enough: we are often afraid of giving space in case we 'lose' or somehow become 'less' of ourselves. But making space for others does exactly the opposite: we become a more impactful and influential version of ourselves, just in a different way.

Although *tzimtzum* is a selfless act, making space for others can bring great fulfilment for you, too. Through the act of making space for others, your personal satisfaction increases. When we stop trying to hog the limelight and instead think about how we can let someone else take centre-stage, it brings humility, confidence and contentment. It helps us manage our lives in a way that frees our soul.

You could get more out of *tzimtzum* than you give away. Because the paradox of making space is that, by contracting yourself, you are even giving *yourself* room to grow. And if you are one of life's people pleasers, someone who feels like they have to fix everything and be everything to everyone, *tzimtzum* will be even more liberating. You don't have to be in full control. You only have to give space.

Tzimtzum

The Hebrew word for 'contraction' or 'concealment'. In the Kabbalah of Jewish mysticism, **tzimtzum** *is used to describe how God created the world.* **Tzimtzum** *is an incredibly holy and complex concept because it describes the process in which God made space for us, His creations. God contracted and concealed a part of His eternal light to make space for His creations: the world and us. We can use this fascinating principle to inspire us in our approach to others. Even when we have the power and authority to take all the space, we should 'contract' ourselves to make space for others: space for them to express different voices, feelings, emotions and ideas. The space we create around us should be free of judgement and ego. Taking up less space allows us to help others grow, and ourselves to grow as well – by learning humility and compassion.*

IF YOU CHANGE NOTHING, NOTHING WILL CHANGE

Tzimtzum is one of the deepest, most profound principles in Jewish wisdom. It is also one of the hardest concepts to grasp and implement because it can feel counterintuitive – how can I grow and help people by constraining myself? One way to start practising **tzimtzum** *right now is by giving yourself the space for reflection. Think about how you could embed* **tzimtzum** *in your life. I invite you to reflect and answer one, two or all of these questions as a way to deepen your understanding of* **tzimtzum***.*

1 Can you think of a meaningful person in your life who gave you the space you needed to grow? In what way was that space helpful?

2 Think about your life right now. Who needs you to give them more space? What would making space for them look like?

3 What purpose or cause do you need to make space for? How will you make space for it?

4 What is an area in your life in which you could practise *tzimtzum*?

5 In which of your relationships (work, family, friends) do you feel there is a healthy 'make space' dynamic? What makes it healthy and how could you embed this in another relationship as well?

7
REPAIR YOUR COMPANY CULTURE

'I've learned that people will forget what you said, people will forget what you did, but people will never forget how you made them feel.'

Maya Angelou

When I first moved to the UK, in the early 2000s, I signed up to an employment agency to help me find a job. After providing information about my education and work experience I was called for an interview. The woman who interviewed me was impressed by my qualifications and experience, but I sensed that something about me was bothering her, so I asked if there was any feedback she'd like to give me. She replied, 'Well, yes, there is actually, and please don't take this personally. I really want to help you, that's why I am telling you this. In this country, ginger curly hair is not the most professional look. If I were you I would consider straightening my hair.'

I instinctively reached up and smoothed my hair. Was it really that bad? Why does this matter at all? No one has ever commented on my hair before. But I nodded and said, 'Of course.'

And there was more: 'And you should know,' she continued, 'that men take women with straight hair more seriously.'

I just wanted to get out of there as soon as possible. I left that interview room so upset, angry and frustrated. Did this woman really think she was doing me a favour? I think the answer was yes, she really did. But the embarrassment of being told I didn't look professional affected me for years. From that time on, I slavishly straightened my hair every day. I wanted to look professional, to fit in, to be accepted.

How could I allow a single comment from a person I had just met affect me for decades? What was so powerful about those words that I felt I had to conform to what people around me wanted me to be? The feeling she had created – in that one conversation – was that I wasn't 'good enough' to succeed.

You're Jewish, Right?

A couple of years later, in one of my roles at an advertising agency, I held a 'networking' meeting for the HR department. The aim was to help everyone get to know each other and share their career experience. After half an hour, when people had started opening up and sharing their backgrounds and career history, we broke up into pairs. A colleague who had recently joined the company said to me, 'So, you're Jewish, right?' I told her I was. 'I've never met anyone Jewish before,' she said, 'but I've heard of the Jewish nose and now I get it.'

I reached up and covered my nose with my hand. I was shocked at what she had said. Being Jewish has always been part of who I am, ancestrally, culturally. Was that unacceptable, too?

Another time, I was working for a major UK bank. It was one of my first high-powered jobs in the UK and I tried my very hardest to add value and succeed in the company. I'd worked above and beyond what was expected of me so, when my half-year review was due, I was keen to receive feedback from my manager.

I sat there nervously as he started reading my formal performance review. 'We're very impressed with your work,' he smiled. I politely smiled back as he listed some of my achievements from the last six months, but as time went on I couldn't help feeling that he was gearing up to some less positive feedback. And then it came.

'But there is one issue,' he said, 'and so I've decided to withhold your bonus for this period.'

What? The job was a base salary with a bonus. It would only be withheld if there was some major shortcoming with an employee's performance. He had just said I'd done a good job. What had I done so wrong? Had I said something hurtful to one of the employees or underperformed on a major project? I couldn't think of anything.

My manager saw the worry on my face and continued, 'You are businesslike and proper, but there is a concern that people in our office may feel uncomfortable with your presentation.' My presentation? I didn't understand. My hair was straight and I wore Zara suits like everyone else. What had I done to offend? He went on. 'It's not that you actually *get* emotional, but we are sensing too much emotion *beneath the surface*. It's not appropriate. We can see that you sometimes feel quite strongly about certain topics and the way you express that doesn't align with our professional standards. Maybe it's a cultural thing, but we do things differently in the UK.'

So my pay was being deducted because I have emotions?

Now, I am not a particularly emotionally expressive person. I very rarely cry. But even if I did, would that make me less 'professional'? I could feel my cheeks burning from the humiliation. I didn't know where to look. He lit a cigarette. He wasn't done yet. (Did I mention he chose to do the review in a pub?) 'And there's one more thing. You move your hands too much when you speak. That's not appropriate.'

I wanted the ground to open up and swallow me whole. But I couldn't possibly react 'emotionally', could I? I just said, 'No problem, this makes total sense. I'll get it right next quarter.'

I'm not proud of it, but as an insecure overachiever, I adjusted my behaviour according to his 'feedback'. I cooled down my 'presentation'. I consciously kept my hands behind my back. And six months later I was rewarded with a full bonus and promotion. I had received the message, loud and clear: I could not be myself and succeed. It was as if I'd been told that, as I was, I was not acceptable. My hair was too curly, my 'presentation' too emotional, my hands too lively and my nose too... Jewish.

And that was just the start of my long career in disguise. I felt I had to put on different masks in different places in order to blend in. The unspoken culture of most of the companies I worked for meant that to be accepted, I had to look and act a certain way.

Have you ever felt like you are putting on a mask when you walk into the office? Or when you meet with a colleague? That others are putting on masks, too?

I wanted to be accepted, badly. But I often wondered whether I chose to join companies that looked good on my CV rather than the ones that would offer the right working environment for me. I realised with sadness that the only workplaces I felt deeply connected to were the charities I volunteered for. There, I was accepted just the way I was. There I felt at home.

When we work for a company that doesn't make us feel safe and cared for, that makes us feel as if we don't belong, it can be a source of pain, much like being rejected by your own family. Yes, we can say, 'It's just a workplace, there's no reason to care that much.' But we do care, and we should! Companies are responsible for creating a safe, inclusive environment for their workforce. It should be a place where people can feel comfortable being who they are, regardless of their age, gender, race, religion or hairstyle. Part of my professional and personal mission is exactly this: transforming the workplace into an inclusive, welcoming 'home' for everyone.

Don't Let Your Soul Get Contaminated

I once worked for a company that had a particularly toxic culture. Unhealthy competitiveness, a lack of transparency among the employees and office gossip seemed to be part of the company's DNA. Every morning I would drag myself out of bed and into the office, knowing that I would face difficult conflicts that would force me into situations where my values were compromised. The toxic environment also caused my own weaknesses to surface, and my ego gained more and more power. I was thinking thoughts that made me feel ashamed of myself, and my anxiety worsened. On paper it was a dream job, but in practice it was the exact opposite. I experienced internal conflict about what I should do: should I stay or go? Was it just that I needed to toughen up and deal with this kind of culture or was it truly toxic and too much to bear? I tried to change the culture for the better. I tried driving towards a more positive workplace, but I wasn't successful.

So I quit. Staying in a culture that was damaging to my inner self was not an option. I knew I was making the right call, because I instinctively felt that the world around me – the culture I lived in day to day – was far more important than my career. I realise I was in a privileged position that unfortunately isn't shared by everyone – not everyone can afford to quit their job – but to me it was clear that no pay cheque or promotion could be compensation enough for the suffering to my inner self. I was in the fortunate position to be able to quit. So I did.

Many years later, when I discovered my soul in the classes on Jewish wisdom – I learnt how each perfect and unique soul is the essence of who we are. It suddenly dawned on me why I found that place so unbearable: *my soul was getting contaminated*. My 'flesh' could deal with the job – it could fake it and play the game – but my soul was being starved of oxygen.

When I was a child, my grandmother Chana – the one who had jumped off the train to Auschwitz – had a nickname for me. She called me *tikkun*. The word literally means 'repair' or 'correct'. For my grandmother, after witnessing all the horrors of the Holocaust, I represented the repair that she needed, a compensation for all she'd lost. I was the new generation, the hope that the world could be a better place.

The Jewish principle of *tikkun* has two facets: personal repair and universal repair, known as *tikkun olam*, which is a pretty well-known Jewish concept. It is the obligation of every individual to strive for personal 'repair' and also to do whatever they can to repair the world.

The more I learnt about Jewish wisdom, the more I realised that I could use many of these ideas to 'repair', correct and improve the environments I lived and worked in. I could play a role in changing the culture around me to make it a better place. And the more I learnt about *tikkun*, the more I realised it wasn't only about changing the world. It was about changing *my* world.

That's the ultimate culture change.

How Do People Feel in Your Company?

The 'culture' around you – the world you are responsible for – doesn't have to be a workplace. It can be your company, or the company you keep – from your colleagues and friends to your family and community. In my career, I've focused on building and nourishing the cultures of large corporations, but every workplace has a culture – from the biggest tech company to your local high street shop. More importantly, every family, friendship, charity, school, club or sports team has a culture, too. Culture evolves any time that people connect together as a group or society. It is through culture that people define themselves within the group, share values and belong. I want to share how *tikkun* can be applied towards building a meaningful culture *anywhere*.

Have you ever stopped to think about the atmosphere you create around you, at home and at work? The kind of culture you have created? And how you could, bit by bit, make it better?

From my own experiences of negative culture, I had come to know that a nurturing environment is one where people can be themselves – where there's no such thing as hair that's too curly or hands that are too expressive. Somewhere everyone has a place and the space to grow.

As you can probably tell, I see similarities between my role at work and my role in my family. I'm not suggesting that your loyalty, commitment or feelings should be the same for your work as they are at home, but it's important to remember that you are the same soul wherever you go. And you shouldn't feel as though you need to put on a mask and pretend to be someone else in order to fit in.

At home and at work, I try to repair my world. I want to share a few ideas with you here, and suggest how, one step at a time, we can improve ourselves and the culture around us.

Show Care to Others

During my first interview at Facebook, the very first thing my future manager asked me was, 'How do you pronounce your name?' In Hebrew, the 'ch' in the middle of my name, Michal, is pronounced as a very guttural 'h'. There is no equivalent in English and it sounds a bit like the noise you would make if something was stuck at the back of your throat. For years I had been resigned to the fact that everyone in the UK mispronounced my name. I even considered changing it to Michelle, to make it easier for everyone. But his question immediately made me feel that he cared. I felt understood. It was a subtle change from the cultures of my previous workplaces, and it hit me powerfully. Everyone else had pronounced my name wrong or avoided saying my name. He had simply asked.

Then, on my first day at work, I was expecting that he'd talk me through my goals and job expectations. I had my tablet open to take notes. But again I was surprised. Instead of setting out his expectations he asked me, 'Michal, what do you care about? What matters to you, at work and in life?' I was taken by surprise. I had worked in many different companies and no manager had ever asked this before.

'Being a mother,' I said. 'Being Israeli and... being Jewish.'

I was immediately scared by my own answer. This kind of stuff was too personal to be sharing at work. It was the equivalent of my curly hair, my gesturing hands; it was too... *me*. Why was I telling my new boss that my family was important, which might imply that I was not fully committed to work? Why was I advertising the fact I was Jewish? But his question had felt so personal that I had instinctively given a very honest response.

'I don't know much about Judaism,' he said. 'Tell me a little more.'

So I told him a few things, including the custom that Jewish women light candles before sunset on Friday night to welcome Shabbat. That Friday evening as I was preparing for Shabbat, I received a text message from my new manager: 'Shabbat Shalom!' And for the next five years he sent me the same message *every single Friday*, without fail. This was such a simple act of care, but it was utterly transformational. It felt like he was saying, 'We welcome you as a whole, including your personal values and lifestyle.'

The way you choose to speak to others has profound ramifications. Sheryl Sandberg, COO of Facebook, shared a moving post after her husband's untimely death, describing, among other things, her return to work and how people can show more empathy to each other:

> A simple 'How are you?' – almost always asked with the best of intentions – is better replaced with a 'How are you today?' When I am asked 'How are you?' I stop myself from shouting, 'My husband died a month ago, how do you think I am?' When I hear, 'How are you today?' I realise the person knows that the best I can do right now is to get through each day.

Showing care is one of the most powerful ways you can repair the culture around you, at work and in life. It costs nothing and takes little time. Care can be found in a thoughtful choice of words, a small gesture or by simply taking into account how another person might be feeling. Another powerful way to express care and build a relationship is by inviting someone to tell you more about what *they* care about, and all it requires is giving them a little space to show your readiness to engage.

Satya Nadella, CEO of Microsoft, once said, 'I'd like to think that the C in CEO stands for Culture.' You might have expected that Nadella, the leader of one of the greatest tech companies in the world, would point to strategy, technology or design as the core of the CEO's role. But that is not the case. What Nadella promotes is the increasing importance of company culture. I'd like to suggest that the C also stands for Care. When you care for others and are cared for, the commitment, love and connection can solve what might previously have seemed unsolvable. And this C is not only in the hands of the company CEO – any employee, friend, partner or parent can help to repair the world by showing care, too.

Have Real Conversations

In my experience, one of the most common challenges in the workplace, and perhaps in life in general, is that people tend to avoid having real, honest conversations. The kind of conversation that builds or maintains trust. Because the stakes are sometimes high, because we'd rather avoid conflict or because it can feel uncomfortable, people often prefer not to discuss important issues. Instead, we hope that somehow things will work themselves out. Unfortunately, that doesn't always happen. And when a conversation that should have taken place doesn't, and things are left unsaid, people end up feeling hurt, disappointed and angry.

So how do you have a real conversation? According to Kerry Patterson, Joseph Grenny, Ron McMillan and Al Switzler, in their book *Crucial Conversations: Tools for Talking When Stakes are High*, we need to approach the conversation with the mindset that the other person is not out to harm us in any way. We should assume their positive intent and make sure we come to the conversation with this approach as well. It's also important to show empathy to the other person, to think about things from their point of view and try to understand what motivates them, what their intentions might be. And, as always, respect is crucial. When we respect the other person, when we are willing to *really* listen to their point of view, and feel able to express our own, we are more likely to manage our emotions effectively. In this way, many misunderstandings can be resolved and the air is cleared. But let's be honest – real conversations are uncomfortable. Both parties feel that way: the person that initiates it to give feedback, as well as the person asked to engage in it.

A while ago, I had a conversation with a former colleague of mine. I hadn't seen this colleague for many years and I was really glad for the chance to catch up, even if only on Zoom. I spoke about my family and the latest news at work, and then I happened to mention a conversation I'd had with a different colleague. 'I spoke about you with Jackie,' I said. 'We both complimented you. I said to her, "He is such a professional and a kind person. I just love working with him."'

My intention was to make a positive comment and I thought this would make my colleague happy, but instead, my colleague looked at me, and, even through the screen, I could sense anger and frustration. What did I do wrong? I thought I was giving a compliment, what did I say that was so upsetting?

'Listen, Michal,' said my colleague. 'I've been avoiding this conversation with you for a while, but now it's time to have it. I know you're not doing this on purpose, but you're hurting my feelings. On my email signature and on all my social media it says very clearly that I identify as they/them. I am not *he*, I am *they*. That's what you should call me.'

I was lost for words and so embarrassed!

I had offended my colleague. I hadn't bothered looking at their email signature. For a very long time I had been speaking to them, and about them, in a way that made them feel uncomfortable, unseen and disrespected.

I didn't know what I should say first: 'Sorry' for hurting you all this time or 'Thank you' for being honest and brave enough to have this real conversation with me. There is a beautiful Jewish saying:

What comes from the heart, goes straight into the heart.

I started with 'Sorry'. I didn't make excuses, I just said sorry. And then I thanked them. They accepted both.

People often avoid meaningful conversations because they worry they won't know what to say or how to say it. They think they need to prepare notes or even a script for such conversations. I want to offer a different perspective. Having real, honest conversations should indeed be done with much thought and care, but the words don't need to be perfect. What comes from the heart, goes straight into the heart. What matters most is to have good intentions, to have respect, to *care*. Try to overcome your wish to avoid tension or conflict. Communicate. Be honest. Very often, once you've had that conversation, you will build more trust, collaborate more effectively and become closer.

At every company I work for, I am known as someone who is not afraid to have a real conversation. In fact, it's one of my strengths, and I consider it a part of my purpose.

As I mentioned earlier, they call me the 'elephant caller', because you can rely on me to point out the elephant in the room, to express what others are thinking but are afraid to say. I don't do it to cause conflict, but to improve relationships and the culture as a whole, and I see it as part of my own contribution to *tikkun*.

Of course, there is another good reason to have real conversations: I want to live a real, honest life, not a shadow of what is real. In a culture where we fear failure and rejection and choose not to be ourselves or speak the truth, good, honest, open relationships simply cannot thrive. But in a culture where people have real conversations, can be themselves and own their feelings, behaviours and mistakes, relationships are deeper, more connected and, yes, more productive.

Real conversations change the culture at home as well. As I write this book, I find myself revisiting old memories, some of them pleasant, some less so. In a way, this process of reflecting on the past is a real conversation I am having with myself. Sometimes it leads to a conversation with others, too. For example, I realised that there are periods in my life I can't remember as well as others. I turned to my beloved younger sister to help me fill in the gaps. I wanted to discover my blind spots and the behaviours I wasn't aware of. I asked her to give me feedback. I received more than I expected when she said, 'Michal, I don't know if you realise this, but for years I couldn't talk to you without feeling intimidated. You made me feel as if you had all the answers. It was hard to meet your high bar. You were so black and white. There was no grey, no middle.'

'Why didn't you tell me this at the time?' I asked. 'Was I that intimidating?'

'Well, you are my big sister, I couldn't challenge you. I preferred to avoid telling you things.'

I think that it was my responsibility as the older sister to create a trusting, safe environment for real conversation, and clearly, I'd failed. But when I got off the phone with my sister, I realised that we'd just had a real conversation, and though there were moments that felt less comfortable, it's these meaningful conversations that will build up our sisterhood and trust.

Having real conversations with your children is really important, too. My teenage daughter has a friend called Zoe who I really adore. I've known her for years and she's always been a great friend to my daughter and a friendly neighbour. One day, when Zoe was visiting us and we were all drinking coffee and hot chocolate together in the kitchen, I was joking with my daughter and said, 'I love Zoe. Maybe we could do a swap for a week – she could come and stay here and you could go and stay at her house. What do you think?'

We all laughed, but my daughter didn't respond right away. It was only after Zoe had gone home that my daughter said, 'Mum, can I tell you something?'

'Of course, darling,' I said, clueless as to what I had done wrong.

'You can love Zoe,' she said, 'but not at my expense.'

For a moment I became defensive, but then I realised what I had done and I apologised. I regretted what I said and how I said it, and I felt bad that I'd hurt her. But then a positive thought emerged. Instead of burying a resentment that would eat into our relationship, my daughter had felt comfortable enough to give me constructive feedback in a respectful way, and the air had been cleared. It was a 'real conversation' and something we could grow from.

Constructive, honest conversations are necessary both at home and at work. They allow us to improve ourselves. Being able to approach these important conversations in a respectful and caring manner is another way to repair yourself and the world around you.

The One Per Cent Feedback Tool

Another way of introducing and maintaining healthy conversations is to give feedback using the 'one per cent tool'. This is a framework that I adopted from multiple sources, including Japanese philosophy and financial models. It's a successful method I use when coaching company leaders and at home. The idea is that ninety-nine per cent of the time we are doing things right. It is only *one per cent* of our output that needs repair and improvement. Obviously, that can't always be true: some people will have more than one per cent to repair, at least some of the time. But if you get too precise with the statistics, you'll miss the point. The overall assumption is that on the whole most of us, most of the time, are doing well.

In my family we have become accustomed to thinking about personal growth through this tool. 'What one per cent can you give me?' is something my children have heard me ask Yair for years. I am known at home and at work for wanting to know how I am doing, how I can improve, to discover my blind spots. Asking for this kind of feedback does not come naturally to everyone, it can feel uncomfortable, even scary. But practice makes perfect.

My family don't just ask for one per cent, we also offer our one per cent to each other – but *only* when we think it is important to make the other aware of something, not as a vehicle for being hurtful. 'Do you want to hear the one per cent?' sends the message, 'I am going to share something you may not be aware of, something small that can make a big difference, but please remember that overall I think you are doing great.' It prevents triggering a defensive response and it places the comments into the context of a positive feedback loop.

My children are now accustomed to giving and asking for feedback, and even though it is a bit uncomfortable, they choose to do it. Not always, only when it feels right. It is in these moments that I truly feel successful as a parent.

Why Are We So Afraid of Failure?

Facebook, like many other tech companies, is a relationship-based company. Building long, trusting relationships is at the core of its internal culture. People don't respect you or do as you ask just because of your seniority or your job title. Job titles don't matter that much, and if you're the kind of person who gets hung up on things like your job title or the location of your desk, you will find it hard to adjust to a non-hierarchical, relationship-based culture. The company leaders sit in an open space like everyone else; they queue for lunch like all the employees do.

One of the companies I worked for previously was exactly the opposite – titles and seniority were everything. Favouritism by senior leaders was your ticket to success. If you asked people too nicely for something or showed too much care, you were perceived as weak and would become a target for backstabbing. It was exactly this kind of culture that makes people afraid to be their true selves, a culture that I wanted to leave behind.

When I joined Facebook I wanted to make an impression, to show that they'd found a good hire in me, that I would deliver results. So when a major project landed on my desk, I was determined to make it a success and, let's be honest, I wanted to be a success too. The project came with high visibility and high priority for my department. At some point the timelines became tight and pressure went sky high. I responded with stress. I started telling people what to do. I wasn't being horrible or offensive, but within this culture of positive relationships, this place that celebrates dialogue and diversity, my voice was too dominant. I got some tough feedback. I'd rubbed a few people up the wrong way and my manager had been made aware. The project landed as a success, but in my eyes, I'd landed as a failure.

In a different company, this overly assertive behaviour might have earned me praise – I would have been seen as someone with authority and guts. But I had moved to Facebook for exactly this reason, so I could be part of a caring workplace that wants you to always grow and be the best version of yourself.

I became worried. Were they going to fire me? Would people stop liking me? I asked for time with my manager and I shared my regret.

'Congratulations!' he said. That was *not* the response I was expecting.

'You landed on your first failure,' he said. 'I can see from looking at you that you're quite upset and I assume you wish you'd managed things differently. That's okay. Take the evening to recover. Then tomorrow morning look at what you've learnt from this experience. Own your mistakes. And you'll be ready for your next project. Just don't repeat the same mistakes – try to make new ones.'

Afterwards, I learnt that my manager had noticed my reaction to the pressure and had even tried to make me aware of it, but I was in my own bubble, and he'd chosen to let me go with it. In other words, he'd let me fail.

This episode helped me realise that one of the best ways to help people and companies grow is to allow them the space to fail. The unspoken 'culture' of my childhood home was that failure was not an option. My parents were well-intentioned of course – they wanted to raise strong, able, successful young women who could manage life's challenges – but good intentions can have unintended consequences and I ended up with a great fear of failure.

Why are we so afraid of failure?

I believe that ultimately it's because we worry that our mistakes will lead to us being rejected. That we will feel broken from our failure – and will look broken to other people. Sometimes the possibility of failing is so horrifying that we avoid important opportunities altogether – we back away from the narrow bridge. We are frightened of humiliation, disappointment, damaging our reputation and letting ourselves (and others) down. But what happens if we build a world around us that not only allows failure, but encourages it?

Fail Harder

My manager 'allowed' me to fail because of the company motto, 'Fail harder'. I have found this to be one of the most powerful motivational messages – both in the workplace and elsewhere, and once I experienced it, it became central to my professional vision. It brilliantly neutralises the fear of failure by sending a compassionate message that failure is okay and will be tolerated, even encouraged. 'Fail harder' makes it clear that failure is a necessary part of growth and that you have to put all of yourself into an endeavour, even if it results in failure. And in the cracks of failure, you may learn something meaningful about yourself.

If you've never been told 'well done' by a manager for *underachieving*, let me tell you, it's a transformative experience. Your operating system learns to say, 'Failure is okay. It's inevitable. It's part of growth. Actually, I should *fail harder* and squeeze the experience for all the incredible value that it contains.' When my manager not only allowed me to fail but told me I would learn from it, I knew I would never make the same mistake again. No one wants to make mistakes, and no manager or company wants their employees to make them. But we are human and, given time, we will eventually get something wrong. What matters most is that we live in a world where we can learn from our mistakes.

Even if your company (or the other cultures you are part of) does not yet embrace failure, you can still recast *your* attitude to it. Indeed, the *Harvard Business Review* published an article by Bill Taylor about the concept of a Failure CV. On this CV, you wouldn't list all the amazing things you have done; you would identify the missed opportunities, all those mistakes you made and – crucially – what you learnt from them. This would reveal far more about who you really are than a regular CV, and indeed, asking about past failures is a standard interview question used by Facebook.

Talking openly about failure isn't intended to bring you down, reduce your confidence or hinder your reputation, it's meant to do exactly the opposite. It's about showing that vulnerability is okay and allowing others to feel that failure is an option, too.

So how could you play your role in repairing the world around you? It could mean improving something for others, such as making space for voices that aren't heard or reducing the focus on yourself and increasing the focus on those around you. Or it could mean repairing your personal belief system, having more real conversations with yourself about where and how you should change, making yourself approachable to others, so they can have these real conversations with you.

Each of us can repair the world around us with our unique strengths, talents and passions. If we better ourselves, we can better things for others. My professional purpose is to inspire and educate companies to improve their company culture, to include everyone as a meaningful part of the workplace community. It's to make employees feel safe, confident and accepted as they truly are, to care for one another, respect each other's uniqueness and to make the company a better place for all.

Tikkun

*In Hebrew, **tikkun** means 'repair' or 'correct'. Repairing ourselves allows us to better repair the culture around us. We must always be aware of the culture we create. The way we act at work, at home or anywhere else can influence how others feel. So think about your own actions and how you can create an inclusive, warm culture around you. Show others that they can be themselves with no fear of judgement or rejection: flawed, quirky, emotional, quiet, passionate – help them remove their masks. Mistakes are okay. Failure is fine. Show the people around you that you care about them. Give feedback in a positive, constructive and compassionate manner. Be honest and speak from the heart – you'll find that if you do it, others will feel comfortable to do the same.*

IF YOU CHANGE NOTHING, NOTHING WILL CHANGE

Whether we are aware of it or not, our presence and how we connect with others will always make people feel something. The same goes for 'culture'. Where there are more than a few people, a culture will evolve. In this chapter we suggested ways to develop a positive, inclusive culture around you. We almost always have an opportunity to repair ourselves so we should use this to extend the repair to the world around us. You are invited to reflect upon and answer the questions here as a way to raise awareness and explore how you could potentially play your part in repair and building positive cultures.

1 How do people feel in your presence? What kind of culture do you create around you?

2 What values and behaviours do you need in the culture around you that will enable *you* to be the best version of yourself? Where in your life do you feel most connected, most cared for?

3 How can you make sure the people around you feel comfortable to take off their identity masks? What can you start doing more or less of to make people feel they can be themselves when they are with you?

4 What real conversations would you be having if you weren't afraid? What are you avoiding?

5 What is the one area in your life at the moment that needs your attention – that you'd like to practise *tikkun* on?

8
LEAD LIKE A MENSCH

'Others wait for something to happen. Leaders help make something happen.'
Rabbi Lord Jonathan Sacks

8

It's a rainy February day and I'm standing at the collection point with my parents, holding my father's hand, surrounded by dozens of buses. Around us are all the other parents and their daughters, taking photos, hugging, making last-minute adjustments to their luggage. I am eighteen, and I am about to leave home. As the rain falls harder I have to say a final goodbye to my mother and father, my sister, girlfriends and cousins, before I get on the bus. I'm distraught at having to leave my parents, but also excited and nervous about the future.

'Good luck,' says my mother, and I kiss her goodbye. I want to make her proud of me.

I'm not going to university or summer camp. I'm joining the Israeli army.

In Israel, most teenage girls know that when they graduate high school at the age of eighteen they'll have to join the military for two years of national service. I also knew this, and I'd been expecting that February day for a couple of years. Now that it was here, although I was terrified of leaving home, I was excited, especially because after the early assessments I had been through during the previous months, it had been decided that I would join the Air Force Intelligence unit.

The Air Force Intelligence unit was more glamorous than the others. The soldiers had a different uniform, a separate kitchen, better food, nicer dorms... and of course there was the chance to hang out with handsome pilots all day (I was eighteen after all). I couldn't believe my luck. All I had to do was complete my basic training and I would be there.

Three weeks of basic training started on the day I waved goodbye to my family. It was an intense initiation into army life. We had to learn how to use and look after our weapon, scrub the enormous pots and pans in the massive kitchen that served thousands of women each day, navigate in difficult terrain and develop the mindset of a soldier. We slept in tents, and the weather was often wet and cold. I remember falling asleep to the sound of two girls sobbing in their beds, from homesickness, exhaustion, or both.

Every morning we had to get our living quarters spotless by 7 a.m. for inspection. If we failed, we would not be allowed to go home for the weekend on a family visit. For most of us, this time off was the only thing that kept us going.

One particular day, no one wanted to clean the toilets. It was no surprise – after all, dozens of girls were using just a few toilet stalls. But that day there was another reason for avoiding this chore: one of the toilets was seriously blocked, and I mean seriously. It wouldn't flush and this made cleaning the unit impossible, and obviously none of the eighteen-year-old recruits wanted to sort it out.

It was getting nearer and nearer to 7 a.m. All the girls were in a panic – the inspecting officers would come any minute and we were nowhere near ready!

I looked around and realised that no one was going to deal with it. So, without giving it too much thought, I went into the cubicle, reached down into the toilet, pulled out the offending item and got rid of it. The entire floor cheered and clapped and some girls even started dancing with their brooms. 'We're going home after all!'

I shouted to their cheers.

As I stood up, I looked behind me and saw... the most senior commanding officer in the base. There I was, my hand still covered with what was left of the blockage, expecting a serious telling off, but she just smiled at me and said, 'You'll be one of us.'

I didn't know what she meant by that until I was called into the commanders' office the next day. They told me that they had re-evaluated my profile and didn't want me to join the Air Force Intelligence unit after all. They have been observing me for three weeks and the toilet incident was the final reassurance for them that I had deep commitment and great care for my fellow trainees, that I was someone who went the extra mile for the team. They said I showed enthusiasm and passion to learn. They wanted me to become a commander.

I was shocked – and disappointed. Me? A commander? I'd never considered that track. What about my dream to hang out with the pilots? That dream had just been flushed down the toilet, too.

Since I didn't have a choice, I accepted my new role and decided to take it seriously. My duty as a commander was to train, educate and discipline new female recruits. These young women were mostly eighteen years old, in some cases just a few months younger than myself, and, like me, had also recently graduated from high school. For most of them, they had never been away from their parents and siblings for more than a few days. In a matter of weeks, I had to turn them from teenagers into soldiers, and teach them how to function in army life. I introduced them to the army's values, principles and mission, trained them on how to use a rifle for self-defence, how to navigate with a map in all terrains, how to use army equipment and how to become part of a team – transitioning their focus from 'me' to 'us'.

After being a commander for less than a year, and following another three months of intense training, I was promoted to commanding lieutenant officer level. My role was the same, but now I was responsible for dozens of women at once, and in addition to commanding them I had cross-unit duties, where a handful of commanders reported to me. At the age of nineteen, taking a hundred women to navigate through deserted territories in the middle of the night was not an easy task. And yet, with the support and belief of my officers (who were probably only nine months older than me) I developed the confidence that I could do almost anything as long as I was willing to train, commit, care and follow guidelines. I was perceived as a highly responsible, committed and talented officer.

But as the saying goes, power corrupts, and as time went on I became rather authoritarian, and the huge responsibility I felt to obey the rules, to stay focused on the goals of our division and to uphold the principles of the army changed something in me. I wanted to be in control, and to appear in control. I wanted to display confidence, to be respected. I was only a year older than most of these women, and I thought my soldiers would respect me less if I showed vulnerability or empathy, though, ironically, these were the very qualities I had been chosen for in the first place.

I was also a bit full of myself. I felt important and powerful. I had zero tolerance for mistakes and I expected my young recruits to become accomplished soldiers in less than a month. I set the highest of standards and, when they weren't met, I expressed my disappointment. Even though just a short while before I had been one of these recruits myself, I cared less about the girls themselves and more about what I wanted them to do. I had lost my empathy.

Many years later, after I had moved to London with Yair, we were invited to a community event by a family we didn't know. I wasn't able to go, so Yair took the children by himself. When he came home he told me that the hosts welcomed him warmly and introduced their children to ours. Yair said they immediately made him feel like part of the family.

'But then something strange happened,' he said. 'At the end of the party the hostess said what a shame it was that you couldn't make it, and that they'd love to meet you, too. She asked about you, where in Israel you're from and what your name is. As soon as I said your name, her face froze. I asked if you already knew each other, and she said that you were in the army together – that, in fact, you were her commander. She said you were the one everyone was afraid of. She said she asked you once if she could take the weekend off to visit her sick grandmother, and you refused. She'd never forgotten it.'

Of course, my husband found this revelation about my past quite hilarious, but I was deeply affected. I cringed when I realised I had been remembered for all the wrong reasons, that I was known in my squadron as a tough, unfeeling leader. Hearing this woman's words reminded me that I wasn't proud of how I led my soldiers in those early days in the military.

Of course, discipline was necessary and rules in the

army are important for unity, fairness and order. It's the same in any company or family: without boundaries and rules we don't know what's expected of us. But I had let my perception of my role's importance get in the way of caring for the people I was leading. I was so concerned with leading with discipline that I forgot to lead with care.

In my defence, as I progressed through my military service, I did adopt a different leadership style. I eventually realised that getting my recruits to follow me through fear didn't get the best out of them or me. I wanted to support them and to find a purposeful role in the army for each of them, that they would want to fulfil. I wanted to lead through inspiration. It took a while, but I eventually understood that leadership wasn't about getting respect through fear. It was about care, empathy and humility.

Be a *Mensch*

'Whatever you decide to do in life, whoever you end up being – just be a *mensch*' is something we often tell our children at home. Being a *mensch* is one of our family values and expectations and its importance is truly second to none. It isn't just us – it's what millions of people aspire to and hope for their children to become.

What is a *mensch* and why is 'being a *mensch*' so important?

Mensch is a Yiddish word and a traditional Jewish idea. It's one of those words that doesn't have a direct translation in English, but it essentially means 'a decent person'. Being a *mensch* means you conduct yourself with care and integrity, you strive for justice, you are fair in your dealings with others, you are modest and humble, and when you relate to other people, you consider what matters to them.

It's interesting that the term *mensch* is one of the highest compliments one person can pay to another, because a *mensch* is by definition modest. Likewise, being a mensch does not depend on achievements or worldly success. And while in our world not every *mensch* is a leader, in an 'ideal' world every leader would be a *mensch*.

So how would a *mensch* lead? By example. By doing more than they ask from others. A leader who is a *mensch* would focus on the job at hand without neglecting the people they work with. A *mensch* is attentive to the needs of those around them, to the reality of their lives. A *mensch* who leads a team at work sees people just as clearly as the year's profits.

When Viktor Frankl was in the Auschwitz concentration camp, he noted that even in that hopeless environment, people always had choices. They could fight for themselves only, or they could choose to help others. He says:

We who live in concentration camps can remember the men who walked through the huts comforting others, giving away their last piece of bread. They may have been few in number, but they offer sufficient proof that everything can be taken from a man but one thing: the last of the human freedoms – to choose one's attitude in any given set of circumstances, to choose one's own way.

And there were always choices to make. Everyday, every
hour, offered the opportunity to make a decision,
a decision which determined whether you would or would
not submit to those powers which threatened to rob you
of your very self, your inner freedom; which determined
whether or not you would become the plaything of
circumstance, renouncing freedom and dignity to become
moulded into the form of the typical inmate.

A *mensch* is always aware of the choices they can
make. And they strive to choose the right thing – not
only for themselves, but for others.

Ego versus Self-Humility

From my experience in the army and later, as a consultant
to senior leaders, I've learnt that one of the biggest
obstacles to being a good leader is ego. Our ego can make
us feel so self-important that we are blinded from seeing
the needs of others. The selfish inclination we talked
about in chapter five, can make us focus too much on
what we need, and not on what we are needed for. As a
leader, what you are needed for is to nurture your people.
It's only when we make space for others by reducing our
ego that we can truly lead.

I previously shared with you some thoughts about
Passover – about how, during this holiday, we remember
the Israelites' slavery in ancient Egypt and how we ourselves
can continue the journey from slavery to freedom by
trying to escape our internal slavery, our own self-imposed

restrictions. But what is holding us back from internal freedom? How can we escape from our own chains today, our personal slavery, our narrow straits?

During the days of Passover, the requirement is that Jewish people don't eat bread; they only eat *matzah*, a specific type of flatbread that contains no raising agent, such as yeast. Any food that contains yeast or has gone through a leavening process is called *chametz* and is forbidden. This may sound like an odd practice: why is *chametz* forbidden? What harm can it do?

Chametz represents our ego. It becomes bloated as it rises, just like self-inflated egoism and pride. *Matzah*, on the other hand, remains flat and unpretentious, symbolising selfless humility. Forbidding *chametz* and removing any trace of it from the house before Passover reminds us that, in order to leave our own internal slavery, we must first tame our ego. By removing anything that puffs us up, we can deflate our ego and open ourselves up to freedom and growth.

Often, we behave in ways that go against our core values simply because we like to puff ourselves up. Never is this more prevalent than in leadership. The power that I had as a young commanding officer temporarily transformed my behaviour and I acted in a way I later regretted. We face the 'Ego Factor' as we climb the ladder at work or enjoy success and influence. But as leaders – both at work and at home – we must try to be humble, to serve others in our leadership, to brush that ego aside and make space for the people we care for.

When I eat *matzah* during Passover I see it as a wake-up call, a reminder, a symbol of humility and humanity. It reminds me that for thousands of years people have been struggling to tame their egos, and that this internal struggle is how our lives are designed to be. It gives me strength and reassurance to know that every time I manage to be a less self-inflated version of myself is a moment of growth. Gaining freedom and breaking out of our personal internal chains is predicated on humility, without puff and fluff. In other words, you don't need to rise physically like the leaven in order to grow inside. On the contrary: growth is dependent on not being trapped by our pomposity.

Meaningful Leadership

You might be thinking to yourself, this is all very interesting, but I'm not a leader. Well, according to Jewish wisdom, we are all called upon to lead in one way or another.

Rabbi Menachem Mendel Schneerson, the Lubavitcher Rebbe, was one of the most influential rabbis of the twentieth century. He is famous for saying that 'everyone must be a leader'. He inspired (and continues to inspire, even after his passing) hundreds of thousands of people to be proactive leaders in their own way. When people think of leadership they often think of others, as if they can't imagine being a leader themselves. But we must shift that perspective. Leading doesn't necessarily mean being a company leader, a general commander or a prime minister. Leading is about believing you have something meaningful to do for yourself, for others and for the world around you. It's about connecting to yourself and others through a purpose, a cause. It's about truly caring, being courageous, being honest and being real.

Parents are leaders. They lead their family and household. They educate and guide the family towards living a meaningful life. They influence their children's lives by connecting them to shared values. They hold themselves responsible and accountable for their family, and they focus on their role day and night. Teachers are leaders, too. They have the potential to shape children's lives and futures, build their outlook on life and guide them to growth. As a mother, I am a leader to my family. I spend a lot of time, care and energy thinking about what each member of my 'team' needs, and how I can support them on their personal path. Whatever role or roles you hold in your private and professional lives, there is always some area where you have the potential to influence others. And where you have influence, you have an opportunity for meaningful leadership.

And *meaningful* leadership is exactly what we are aiming for. Because what is the point of leadership if not to create meaning? Leadership isn't only about steering your company through change or new strategy. It's not just about telling your children what time to be ready in the morning or helping them do their homework. True leadership is where we can impart the wisdom of our own experiences in a constructive way – where we can bring *meaning* to the journey by focusing on a shared purpose.

We've already established how important it is to find your purpose, to discover what you are here to do, to understand what your unique mission is, today, right now. As the expression of your purpose changes and evolves, you grow as a person, *and* as a leader.

So why do so many of the leaders I've worked with respond in the same way to the question: What is your purpose? What meaning do you lead for?

'Meaning? Purpose? I wish I had one.'

It may be that we are afraid to identify our purpose, to even look for what's meaningful to us. Many of us are wired to focus on tasks, on to-do lists, on 'stuff', on being busy. We fear asking ourselves the questions – Why am I *really* here? What am I *really* here to do? It's a complicated fear. It's a fear of not finding purpose and, at the same time, a fear of finding it and then not being able to 'unsee' it. That's the thing with finding your purpose: once you see it, you must act upon it.

I think I know what you're about to ask. It's a question I am asked often, and something I ask myself, too: How should we act on our purpose? How can we start leading meaningfully? I want to share some of the ideas that have helped me take action. It all starts with remembering the idea of the *mensch*. And then it takes courage. Courage can mean all sorts of things to all different people, but the most fundamental type of courage is the courage to be yourself.

Take Off Your Armour

I've consulted with leaders at all levels and in all areas of their organisations. From VPs of tech and sales, startup founders and CEOs, to heads of industry and board directors. I also consult with leaders of non-profit organisations as part of my voluntary work. Seeing some of these leaders wearing their external personas for the media and then meeting them one-on-one and hearing what they truly care about and believe in helps me understand the gap they've created between who they really are and who they think they should be in public.

There is no reason for anyone to need two personas. You are one person, and the same person whatever you do and wherever you are. Developing different versions of yourself won't bring you joy, confidence or satisfaction. If you are a better version of yourself at home, in your personal life and with your friends, why should you change yourself for your workplace or job? Why not be that better person all the time? Why do many of us leave our true selves at home and wear a mask when we transition to our 'work' persona?

What are we afraid of?

My time in the army taught me that I didn't need to be someone else when leading. I had to lead as myself. Later, when I discovered Jewish wisdom, I learnt how to grow the real qualities required for leadership, and how, when we develop clarity on who we are, what we stand for and how we help others to grow, we naturally become better leaders.

And yet this still goes against how too many people view leadership. As Jacinda Ardern, the prime minister of New Zealand said:

> One of the criticisms I've faced over the years is that I'm not aggressive enough or assertive enough, or maybe somehow, because I'm empathetic, I'm weak. I totally rebel against that. I refuse to believe that you cannot be both compassionate and strong.

Jacinda Ardern is an inspiring example of a leader who hasn't taken on the persona that's expected of her. She demonstrates that vulnerability and strength can live side by side. That staying true to yourself and being a powerful leader are not mutually exclusive.

Remember that manager who took away my bonus because I was 'too emotional'? I'm not sure I would accept his behaviour today. Not when we have leaders like Adern who make it very clear that being caring, compassionate, humble and vulnerable *is* being strong. In *Dare to Lead: Brave Work. Tough Conversations. Whole Hearts*, Brené Brown talks about 'taking off our armour'. She explains that this is how strong business leaders demonstrate effective leadership and motivate teams.

At a 2019 conference, Brown spoke in more detail about this idea. She said, 'How can you be brave if you don't put yourself out there? You can't... If you build a culture where vulnerability is seen as a weakness, don't ask people to innovate because innovation by its nature requires failure, to learn and move forward. Vulnerability is showing up without your armour.'

Courage is a core human trait that each of us possesses. It is something we are born with, that naturally resides inside us. The question is, how do we use it to lead?

Leading with courage means applying our strength to protect and stand up for those who need us, including ourselves. We practise courage whenever we leave our comfort zone, take an unpopular stand, expose our vulnerabilities or speak the truth. We demonstrate courage when we intervene on behalf of those unable to do so for themselves. When we aim to repair what needs repairing, ourselves included.

Once you know that you are gifted with courage at birth, taking a stance as a leader and doing what's right will feel less intimidating or scary.

Courage is not about denying or repressing fear. Rebbe Nachman of Breslov thought that courage is choosing not to frighten ourselves beyond the fear we already experience. Some portion of fear is unavoidable, perhaps even required. Courage involves moving forward despite our fear, and not exacerbating it. Leaders cross bridges. They cross them first and soon after others follow, either on the same bridge or on their own personal bridges – moving forwards, always, with courage and purpose.

Build a Place for Belonging

Jewish wisdom is very clear on this fact: humans were not created to live in isolation from one another. They were created to do just the opposite, to connect with each other. Humans are meant to feel safe knowing that they are valuable members of a community, members of a family, part of something greater than themselves. This is probably one of the reasons the Covid-19 pandemic was challenging to so many of us: it imposed isolation, which goes against the very core of what it is to be human. It is no surprise that we saw old and new communities getting together in new ways, connecting through technology and finding all sorts of creative ways to engage with each other. As we said previously, sometimes from the brokenness can grow something new and whole.

Because being a part of something bigger is so universally and deeply important, part of your role – as a leader, as a human – is to make space for people to belong. That place has to be welcoming, accepting and completely without judgement.

Meaningful leadership is leading for your people, offering them a sense of belonging and a shared purpose. Most importantly, people need to feel included and accepted. Being a part of a larger group (a home, workplace, religion, club, sports team, etc.) grounds us, comforts us, gives us joy and offers opportunities for connection. Wherever you lead, your role involves building that community as a place to belong. Your aim should be that no one feels like they have to 'wear' a persona to fit in. 'Fitting in' is not part of the jargon, instead the word is – belonging.

Be Present

One of the simplest, yet most profound ways to make people feel safe, that they belong, is to be 'present'. To show that you see them, that you care about *them*. People can always tell if you are truly present or not. They will pick up on whether you are with them, in the moment, invested in them and in their unique needs and expectations, or if you are distant, distracted, just thinking about yourself. They will know whether they matter to you, and if you truly care for them. Leaders who fake showing care by asking a question and then looking at their phone or laptop show that they don't really care. This can hurt the relationship more than if they hadn't asked the question in the first place. A true *mensch* would never do that!

One of the leaders who inspired me over the years used to ask me simple, open ended questions about what matters to me and what is meaningful in my life right now. And then – crucially – they'd *listen* to my answers with their full attention. They would ask me insightful, personal questions that made me pause, reflect and ask myself, 'Is this what really matters to me?' or 'Am I focusing on the right thing?' Their behaviour made me feel cared for and it also helped me grow my own self-awareness. This was truly a gift to me, and it reminded me that being present is a present.

Life can sometimes feel like 'a lot'. A close colleague used to say that there's a sense of 'Too Muchness' in how we live our lives – too much expectation, too much opportunity, too much internal pressure – everything is just, *too much*. When Covid-19 broke out there was a new 'Too Much': too much uncertainty. When there's so much going on, when it feels like we're drowning in too much 'muchness', we often choose to disconnect. It's our way of coping when things get overwhelming. But one of the expectations of a good leader is to be the opposite of this – to be present. Meaningful leaders connect. They are deeply involved, they feel, breathe, understand and relate to the reality they are operating in.

Have you ever caught yourself not being present enough when you should have been? How did you feel after realising you were not fully present when another person was talking to you, needing your attention? How could you transition to be more present, more often?

Being present is a present, both for you and for the people around you. This applies at work, at home, in the community, with your siblings, your parents and with your spouse. When someone doesn't appear present, people don't feel listened to, they don't feel validated. This doesn't mean that you need to be physically in the same room in order to be present for someone. There are ways to be present from the other side of the globe. Yes, it is more challenging, but that's exactly why leaders need to be more present than ever.

Be Self-Aware

You should also be present with yourself. Read your reactions to different life situations. Assess your body language. Reflect on how you respond to different people, to different challenges. Self-awareness is key for effective leadership and so is awareness of others. Awareness of how you make others feel, think and believe.

Only once you're fully present and honest with yourself can you be attentive to others. In particular, be aware of your reactions to comments, events or situations that bring out the less empathetic version of you. Knowing your weaknesses will enable you to identify the things that cause you to act in ways you will later regret. This is the first step to being able to better manage how you deal with those challenges that will inevitably arise.

Practising self-management is fundamental to meaningful leadership. This doesn't mean that you stop yourself from being creative, from feeling, learning or making mistakes. It means that you have to be in charge of yourself, to be accountable for your actions, before you can start doing the right thing for everyone else – before you can start leading like a *mensch*.

Lead Towards Justice

A big part of being a good leader is doing the right thing for others, for the world. The English word for charity comes from the Latin word *caritas*, meaning 'dear.' The message is: giving to others is an expression of love for them. We've come to think of charity as optional. In Judaism, charity has a different meaning. In Hebrew, the word for charity is *tzedakah*. This comes from the term *tzedek*, which means 'justice', 'integrity', 'fairness' or 'righteousness'. *Tzedek*, therefore, is quite different to *caritas*. It implies that giving isn't just a nice thing to do, it's the *right* thing to do. As if, through giving, you correct the imbalances of society. Furthermore, it's more than voluntary, it's almost as if failing to give charitably is an *injustice*.

Charity isn't just about money, but correcting the injustices of society in other ways. We each have a responsibility and accountability to act for justice, to correct what is wrong. Even the person that has less to give is expected to do what they can to drive for greater justice, whether that's giving time, advice or anything else they can offer someone less fortunate. That's why charity is not only an act of kindness, it's the *fair thing to do*. And it brings meaning to all involved.

As a leader, the idea of making things right should be your north star. Let it guide you when you make decisions and when you are in conflict. Think about what you are needed for, rather than what you need. Think of what the world – your immediate, personal world and also the wider world – needs from you. And give generously.

As US Vice President Kamala Harris said on the night her election was announced:

'I'm thinking about her [her mother] and about the generations of women – Black women, Asian, white, Latina and Native American women – throughout our nation's history, who have paved the way for this moment tonight. Women who fought and sacrificed so much for equality, liberty and justice for all.'

As a white woman who's been raised in a relatively safe environment by parents who provided me with an education and other opportunities, I know I am privileged. This puts me under a great, sacred obligation – to recognise injustice when I see it and to do whatever is in my power to raise awareness and actively promote a just society. I see my role as a leader, a mother and an educator to make that change happen, right now, because, as it says in *Ethics of the Fathers* 1:14:

If I am not for me, who will be for me? And if I am only for myself, what am I? And if not now, then when?

Charity and Justice

The Hebrew word for 'charity' comes from the same root as the word for 'justice' or 'righteousness'. Giving to charity isn't just something nice we do when we think of it, it is the right thing to do. We shouldn't look at it as optional, it should be part of our everyday thinking. In the same way, we should strive to be a **mensch** *– a good person. Being a good person isn't optional, it should be part of our everyday thinking. As leaders, we should seek fairness and justice for those who rely on us. Everyone has the potential to be a leader – at home, at work, in the community. Leading meaningfully, towards a shared purpose, for justice, while connecting people together, is something we can all do.*

IF YOU CHANGE NOTHING, NOTHING WILL CHANGE

There are tens of thousands of books written about leadership out there – how to motivate, influence and drive others for performance and great engagement. This chapter, and this book, have a different purpose and focus. Instead of thinking about what you should do to people, we start and focus on the most fundamental requirement of leadership: how to be a 'person', and how to lead like a **mensch**. *I invite you to answer one, two or all of these coaching questions in order to take another step in your leadership development. What is most important is that you stay curious, open and honest with yourself. Self-reflection itself is growth.*

1 Who has been a *mensch*-like person in your life so far? What have you learnt from them?

2 What is your strongest human quality? What are your *mensch* behaviours that people are drawn to?

3 What are the comments, events or situations that cause you to be less empathetic? At home? At work? How could you manage them more effectively?

4 How can you be more charitable in your life? Where can you have an impact and bring about more justice and fairness?

5 In what area of your life do you want to lead meaningfully? What could be a first step?

9
GUIDE YOUR CHILDREN BY THE SOUL

'Parents can only give good advice or put them [children] on the right paths, but the final forming of a person's character lies in their own hand.'

Anne Frank

Although I have served as an army officer, consulted with managers and leaders and been a manager myself, my most meaningful leadership role so far has been as the leader of my family. Leading my family – building our home culture, our values, our ways of communication, trusting and caring for each other – is definitely my most fulfilling leadership job. And it is not just a big responsibility, it's a daily learning experience, too. It's a 24/7, permanent position.

Until I had my own family, I measured my 'value' through the eyes of my parents. Like most children, I learnt how to read and interpret their body language and their responses to what I said or did. I worked out what pleased them and what disappointed them in my behaviour. Everything I did or said, and in many ways even my thoughts, was filtered through my parents' expectations. I never really challenged or disobeyed them. Most of the decisions I made – about who to date, what to study at school, in which unit to serve in the military and what profession to choose – were aimed to please them. After all, their parents had gone through the horrors of the Holocaust and survived, they'd worked hard to build our family and to provide for us, the least I could do was to make them happy and proud. I wanted to be perfect for them.

There was never any question in my mind that I wouldn't follow an academic path. Both my parents are highly educated and, if the Holocaust had taught them anything, it was that you had to make yourself indispensable to the world. In our family, we did that through education.

But when it was time to register for university after my three years of military service, I had no idea what I wanted to study. I didn't know what subjects I loved. I had never asked myself that question. Deep down, I wanted to become an actress. I loved watching movies and reading plays, imagining the characters' lives and thoughts. I would stand in front of the mirror and pretend I was on stage, acting, getting inside the characters' heads. I also loved dancing and would spend a few hours a day dancing by myself, improving my moves and the flow of that day's choreography. But when I asked my parents how I could improve my acting and dancing and possibly make it my profession, their reaction was clear: 'You don't want to have the life of an actress, Michal. You want to have a normal, balanced life. You won't be able to be the mother and wife you want to be.' And that was that. I never got to the big stage, never became an actress or a dancer. The dream was gone.

Instead, I chose a combined business and academic path and decided that I would go for a degree in law. It was a solid, respectable, useful profession and I knew my parents would approve of it. I was accepted to the university I applied for. As I was preparing to start my first year at university, I was making a list of all the books I needed for my course. I suddenly looked down at this list and wondered: why have I signed up to study this? Do I *really* want to practise law? I tried to imagine the day-to-day reality of studying and practising law and I realised I was about to make a big mistake. But how could I tell this to my parents? I knew I couldn't become an actress, but now I also knew I didn't want to be a lawyer. Would I ever find my *thing*?

I pulled out of law school. It must have been a higher power that gave me the courage and strength to change my mind because there were serious consequences. There was the money already laid out for the semester, plus I had to take a year out because the application deadline for all the other courses had passed. I decided to spend the year waitressing and applied for a degree in Sociology, Anthropology and Gender Studies.

My parents' reaction to this sudden change of heart surprised me. They were supportive. I came to understand that the expectations were mostly mine – I had my own 'story' of what they wanted me to study. When I reminded them about their reaction to my actress dream a few years back, they didn't remember it at all. It's funny that just a single, casual comment from them stuck with me for years. That's a lesson I took with me for life – when you say something as a parent, it can impact how your child thinks for a long time.

Anyway, I loved Gender Studies! Once I'd completed my bachelor's degree, I decided to continue my studies towards a master's degree in Organisational Sociology and then another master's in the field of Psychoanalysis. Over the course of ten years, I studied while working to support myself – and I found that working and studying full time took my mind off my constant anxiety.

Did the world miss out on the next Scarlett Johansson or Nicole Kidman? I don't think so. Was I talented enough to become a professional actress? Probably not. But was there another way? A middle way that would have allowed me to keep on dancing and acting and fulfilling my passion? I assume there was.

It's Out of Your Control

As I've mentioned earlier, getting married took a leap of faith for both me and Yair, and it brought about new fears. But during my first pregnancy, I suffered from two additional kinds of anxiety. One, that something would go wrong with the pregnancy or birth, and the other, a huge sense of responsibility and fear about bringing a human being into the world and raising her to become a happy, strong woman.

During that first pregnancy my overall grand plan was this: I would be in CONTROL.

This outlook was also built on the views I had learnt during my psychoanalysis studies, which included an introduction to behavioural psychology. This branch of psychology, which was established in the UK in the 1960s, claims that a child is basically a blank canvas and the painting of that canvas is *entirely* the result of parental conditioning. I thought that, effectively, I was fully responsible and accountable for the kind of person she would turn out to be. Any mistakes I made would harm my child, possibly permanently, and require years of therapy later in life.

You can imagine how that made me feel. It was all on me. It was not only my full responsibility to keep this baby alive, healthy, fed, bathed, content and happy, it was *also* my full responsibility to make her a perfect human being. The weeks leading up to her birth were full of anxiety and fear. How was it possible to control who she is and who she becomes? And poor baby! Her mother is so far from perfect, she will have no chance of becoming perfect herself.

Throughout the nine months, horrible visions kept passing through my mind of all the possible things that could go wrong. I started imagining threats that weren't really there to the point that they became real. Most expectant mums attend antenatal classes to prepare for the birth, but I wasn't able to do that; the classes would simply have fed my anxiety with further scenarios of disaster that I hadn't yet contemplated. I booked a planned caesarean delivery. I needed to be in control.

I was so unprepared that, when my waters broke, I didn't really know what was happening. When I was admitted to hospital, I asked for the caesarean I had reserved and was shocked when my request was denied. They said, 'Ma'am, you're going to push like everyone else.'

A Mother's Fear of Failure

When my daughter was born, I remember looking at her, worried that I would fail her as a mum. She was so delicate and fragile. It turns out I failed her almost immediately: one of the most traumatic experiences of my life was my complete failure to breastfeed my first child. All the other new mums on the ward were gushing milk, and I was dry. My baby screamed day and night because she was hungry. I felt so inadequate. She had just been born and I was already disappointing her.

It is so easy as a parent to fall prey to bad thoughts. All of us are susceptible to feeling helpless and exhausted; some of us suffer from anxiety or postnatal depression, and almost all new mothers have to deal with hormone imbalances, which make early parenthood a very difficult time. My daughter was in my arms, screaming for milk that I didn't have. I know now that my body – and probably hers too – was adjusting to this new reality and I just needed a bit more time. But I had disappointed myself and feared I was already disappointing my three-day-old daughter. I cried almost non-stop. But often, just when everything seems dark and hopeless, this is exactly when a new light shines. In this instance, hope came from an unexpected place – from my dear father.

My father is a man who doesn't often show emotion. But in that hospital, he showed his inner self. He stroked my baby's tiny head, looked at her with tears in his eyes and said, 'Another miracle.' I started crying. I felt like such a failure, a mother without milk, and here was my reserved father reminding me that I was his miracle. He held my hand with his warm, delicate, professor's hands and, although he avoided my eyes, he saw into my broken heart. He intuitively understood my fear and pain and said, 'Michal, your daughter will grow to be a wonderful girl regardless of what milk she drinks – yours or formula. What she needs is a happy mother, and you're not happy now. Give her a bottle, go to sleep and everything will be fine.' And that's what I did. I didn't breastfeed my firstborn. And she grew up to be everything my father promised she would be.

This was one of the strongest parenting moments I experienced as a daughter. My father assured me that I would be a good mother and that the known and unknown challenges ahead of me could be overcome. Donald Winnicott, a British paediatrician and psychoanalyst, coined the phrase 'Good Enough Mother' in his 1953 book, *Playing and Reality*. Winnicott found that babies and children don't need a 'perfect' parent or carer in order to become healthy, happy young people. His surprising findings showed that babies actually benefit when their mothers fail them *in manageable ways*, and in some cases may grow more from their parents not rushing to them the second they need something. This might mean not changing a nappy the moment it is full or responding instantly when a baby starts crying. These small and measured delays that cause minor frustrations actually help the baby develop well and adapt to the world.

I learnt that being 'good enough' means that you are still caring, loving, supportive, but at the same time you don't meet every single expectation your child may have. It means that your child won't always get what they want or what they think they need. And those delays or 'dissatisfying' experiences actually help the child develop because – let's be honest – life doesn't always live up to what we want from it. When I read about the 'Good Enough Mother' I realised that I needed to take the word 'perfect' out of my new motherhood vocabulary.

Their Path, Not Yours

Fast forward seven years, and by now I had not one child to worry about, but three. At this point I had already let go of my perfection fantasy, but I was still parenting my children with the belief that my role was to tell them who they are and who they should become. I still assumed they were born a 'blank canvas' and that it was up to my husband and me to draw on that canvas and paint their path for them.

I was searching to learn the essence of being a parent. I approached a friend whose parenting I found inspiring, and she shared a piece of parenting advice from a rather unusual source: the third king of Israel, King Solomon.

King Solomon, who reigned during the tenth century BCE, was famous for his great wisdom. He composed classic biblical books, including *Proverbs*, *Song of Songs* and *Ecclesiastes*. How exciting it was to discover that this great king had advice on how to parent. These are his words on how parents should help their children grow:

> *Teach a child according to his way; even when he grows old, he will not turn away from it.*
> Proverbs 22:6

When I first read these words – possibly the oldest parenting advice on the planet – I thought I had misread them. The essence of parenting that King Solomon describes here is so very different from how I, or most of the other parents I know, had been parenting. It says that instead of steering our children into the people we think they should become, we should teach them according to their nature.

Educate Your Child

As you know by now, the ancient Hebrew language holds great significance and meaning in its combination of letters and words. Often there isn't a straightforward translation of certain Hebrew words for exactly this reason. The word *chinuch* is used in general, everyday conversation to mean 'education'. However, there is a much deeper meaning to the word – one that reveals the absolute essence of the act of educating.

The root of the Hebrew word *chinuch* literally means 'initiation' or 'inauguration'. In the Torah, the word is used to describe the act of dedicating people (or even objects) to their particular purpose. Different objects were dedicated for different purposes. What do these ideas have to do with education? As a parent, your role is to initiate and dedicate your child to their particular purpose. Each child has their own unique potential and talents. When we educate them, we should try to think about who they are and teach them in a way that will ignite *their* passions, inspire *their* curiosity and speak to *their* talents.

I should say that, at this point, I knew that my parenting method wasn't successful. I felt frustrated and exhausted. I was in constant conflict with one of my children in particular. I felt embarrassed at the level of arguments I sometimes had with my children. I wasn't able to keep myself out of some of the dynamics and I got too emotional, too often. I thought it was my duty to show each of them 'the way' and get them on the right track, and felt frustrated when I failed to do so.

Surprisingly, this almost 3,000-year-old piece of advice appeared to be telling me that a parent's role isn't to 'fix' their children or to define for them an exact track, but rather to help them discover their own paths in life.

It seemed to suggest that each child has a predefined journey that they need to discover *themselves*, and a parent's role is to *guide* their children, not to mould them. I realised that my children already had *their own way*. In fact, like me, they'd been born with it. Children are not 'blank'. They each have a unique soul, which carries its own purpose on Earth. Each unique soul is preprogrammed with its own approach to living and to loving, each soul has arrived here for its own personal journey.

I saw that I wasn't helping myself, or my children, when I was raising them all to fit one mould, my mould. I was giving all my children the same guidance, and having the same expectations of each of them. It was not going to work. They were all my children, but clearly they were not all the same. They were not like me, or my husband, or each other, and nor should they be.

This idea – that our children are unique, preprogrammed and autonomous – is one of the most important truths I've learnt and one I deeply care about sharing. It has helped me both to parent all four of my children and also to be parented, later on, by my own mother and father after sharing this with them. I have learnt that my role is to help each of my children grow 'according to their way'.

Does this mean I should sit back and allow my child to choose a dangerous or self-destructive path? Or that I now have no expectations for them? Absolutely not. They must be encouraged to forever grow and develop in a positive way while journeying along their own positive paths.

Telling your children that they have a unique path to

follow, and that you will help them find it, will make them feel special and one of a kind – just as they really are.

One of the Chassidic principles I often remind my children of – on their birthday or on any day they need to hear it – is:

The day you were born is the day God decided that the world was missing you.
Rebbe Nachman of Breslov

This message is so important and encouraging. On the day of your birth, the world needed exactly *you* and that is why you were born. You are here for a reason, and your job is to find out what that reason is.

Although we are talking mainly about children in this chapter, this applies to you too. *You* are here because the world needs you. Ask yourself, in the context of parenting and being parented: What is your role? What are you here to be and to do?

Being your child's guide is not easy or straightforward. There is still uncertainty, frustration and concern. At times you will need to be more involved in your child's path and their decisions, and at others, it's better to step back. The challenge is understanding when. The good news is that there's no need to map out your child's future. That will come about naturally after your child finds their way.

While I was writing this book, my eldest daughter had to have an emergency operation. As I sat by her hospital bed, she described her anxiety at the suddenness with which her illness required an operation. I knew then that, although I was far from being the perfect mum, I was absolutely the perfect mum for *her*. I was the right person to understand and contain her feelings, just as she was exactly the right child for me.

How often do you stop and ask yourself: Who is my child? What do *they* need from me in order to blossom as a human being?

I now know from my own experience that my children were never a blank canvas. When they were born and I looked deep into their eyes in those precious moments of connection, their souls started to unfold, and I began the never-ending journey of getting to know each of them.

Make Space for Your Child

After raising three children as an anxious mum, I was given another chance. By the time I gave birth to my fourth, I had learnt that parenting wasn't all about me. In fact, I had learnt that nothing was all about me. I had evolved as a parent and learnt how to step aside. This coincided with my discovery of *tzimtzum* – the idea that we can and should 'contract' ourselves to make space for others. Now I wanted to practise *tzimtzum* as a parent and make space for my children so they could discover their path for themselves.

Practising *tzimtzum* in parenting is essential. Contracting yourself to make space for your creation is a beautiful act of love and kindness. Contracting yourself so your child has space to grow will ensure that they not only feel safe and secure, but that they become the people they were meant to be. The space that a parent creates for their child isn't an empty box that the child needs to fill. It's not a space that holds uncertainty. It's a space for growth and discovery, a space that can be filled with joy and development, as well as with failure and challenge.

So how do we practise *tzimtzum* with our children?

There isn't a quick tip or answer to this question. Personally, I believe that children need clear boundaries to offer safety and certainty. The space within the boundaries is a safe space for growth. Only you can define your family boundaries, your values, your culture. This means that as parents we guide them with all the wisdom and knowledge we have, that we model good behaviours and care for others, and then we take a step back, and make space.

Yes, we are always present, but we don't want to take up all the space. Being present does not mean that you have to physically be with your child all the time. It means that they can sense your presence, your care, even if you are not there with them. I would never let my child put themselves or others at risk with their choices, but as soon as it's clear they are ready, I want to encourage them to start making decisions for themselves. Observe your child's confidence – you know them best. You will learn when to hold on and when to let go. Model sensitivity and emotional intelligence, look them in the eye in a supportive way and, most importantly, show them that you trust them. This can feel scary, believe me, I know. I am the parent that follows the news when they go out on a school trip, fearing an accident, God forbid, or a terror attack. But we have to let go.

Making space for your children also includes making space for their emotions, especially when they don't have enough space inside themselves for big feelings. It was just after I'd heard of King Solomon's advice and learnt the concept of *tzimtzum* that I came across another idea from Donald Winnicott that got me really excited. It just connected everything for me. In addition to the 'Good Enough Mother', Winnicott talks about a mother being a 'container' for her children. This means that, when a child goes through intense emotions, the kind that seem too big for the child to cope with, the mother can 'contain' those big feelings within herself by offering comfort, understanding and acceptance. This allows the child to experience the emotion fully without feeling overwhelmed. It's nothing more than the way she looks the child in the eyes, how she speaks to them: being warm and making them feel safe. The space that a mother creates for the overflow of feelings allows the child to experience difficulties in a safe way. Parents do these things quite naturally when they comfort a child, when they reassure them that 'next time you'll get it right,' when they say, 'I am here for you.'

Making space for your children will also mean letting them experience failure. No one wants their child to fail and you shouldn't look for it to happen, but if it happens – and it will – you have the power to turn it into a learning experience for them and help them grow.

Choose the Flavour of Your Home

As I mentioned before, making space for your children doesn't mean that you take a passive approach to parenting. Whatever you do, don't be a 'vanilla' parent and fail to give your children the guidance and direction they need. Children require that support. You are the leader of your family, *you* create the family culture, the family values, the belief system. Creating a positive culture at home will make your children feel safe. They will understand what connects you as a family unit, and they will be aware that your family has its own unique soul.

Helping your child find their path is done within the context of your family values. Your family dynamics as well as your relationship with your spouse or other family members will naturally evolve into a kind of 'culture'. You can shape the culture to include the values that you wish. Children grow confident when there is a positive structure around them, when they know what to expect from themselves and their parents, and what is expected of them. They need to *always* feel safe, loved and protected by us, their parents. That doesn't mean that we need to solve their problems for them. It means that we should aim to be by their side, guiding them, holding their hands, but not living life for them: that is *their* task.

Being a vanilla parent means that you miss opportunities to create meaning with and for your children. Creating meaning at home will eventually help you raise confident children.

So how can you bring more meaning to your home? One way to start is to choose three or four core values that resonate with you and start applying them consistently. You are the chef and you can decide the flavour of your home. You can *repair the world* of your family by instilling the values that mean something to you. Having a clear vision of what your family aims to be should guide *everything* you do. Your children will thank you one day, even if that day feels quite far away.

Over the years, as Yair and I have partnered to create the unique flavour we want for our home, we have explored many different ways to guide and nurture our children. Some were successful, others were less so. I want to share with you some of the concepts and ideas that I feel have helped us shape the culture of our home.

Focus on their Souls, Not their Academic Success

Jewish wisdom perceives life as a journey.

It's a journey of the soul.

The discovery of Jewish wisdom has helped my husband and me make some major decisions. We debated our options, we considered our parenting 'strategy'. We decided that developing our children's souls, personalities and humanity, would *always* come before their academic or professional achievements. That is our focus. Of course you can combine all of those, but our priority is very clear. We believe that is the absolute foundation to living a purposeful life.

We have chosen to structure our family values on the principles of Jewish wisdom, many of which are shared by other religions and societies: respect, kindness and honesty are at the core of our family culture. Our children are praised if they demonstrate these behaviours and will be informed if they miss too many opportunities to demonstrate them. For example, if they do not call their grandparents before Shabbat to give their love and best wishes, if they speak disrespectfully to a friend or if they jump off their chairs without helping us clear the table. I used to think I could never get my children to do those things, but I have, and they've done it ever since I started practising meaningful leadership at home.

These values are our guiding light when we make 'educational' decisions. As organisational psychologist Adam Grant says in his article 'Stop Trying to Raise Successful Kids', your success as a parent is not determined by whether your children get into elite schools or prestigious professions: 'The real test of parenting is not what children achieve, but who they become – and how they treat others.'

In other words, we want each of our children to grow up to be a wholesome person – or in Grant's words, a 'giver, not a taker'. One of my children's schools considers this such an important quality that it has a 'Mensch of the Month' award, ranked on equal footing with academic achievement. I love this! It's an award that truly holds meaning. Parents, teachers, businesspeople – let's try to promote 'The Giver Award' or the 'The Kindness Award'.

I once heard a story about the early twentieth-century leader, Rabbi Yosef Yitzchak Schneersohn. As a teenager, he was once taking a walk with his father in the woods. He ripped a leaf from a tree, absently tearing it up with his fingers as he walked along. His father chided him, explaining that every leaf is invested with divine life, a spark from God, who created it. This was a life-changing moment for the young Yosef Yitzchak, when he learnt that he must be aware of how he acts towards everything around him, even a tiny leaf. The lesson stayed with him as he grew up to be a great rabbi and leader.

I told this story to each of my children, each in a separate moment when I felt that they needed to learn this lesson. They adopted the idea so beautifully. Initially, they implemented it literally, by stopping themselves from pulling up the grass in our garden. 'What did the grass ever do to you?' they started asking each other if one of them pulled up grass or a flower. But as time went on they also understood the need to exercise this restraint in relationships as well. I can see this when I watch them stop and think before they are about to say something mean or hurtful, or when I see them consider any unintended consequences to their everyday actions.

As a parent, it's important to help your child to not just develop respect for good values, but to want to uphold them too. 'When I grow up I want to be a *decent person.*' It shouldn't matter if they are a doctor, lawyer, shopkeeper, therapist or actor; what matters is that they play their own role in repairing the world and themselves. These are values children are never too young to learn.

The 'Compliments' Game

One of the most meaningful gifts I gave to myself and my family is deciding to observe Shabbat. Shabbat is the Jewish day of rest. From sundown on Friday until nightfall on Saturday, Jewish people are required to refrain from work, so Shabbat gives me twenty-five hours each week without phone calls, emails, television, shopping, travel, household chores or errands. I have the time and space to truly reflect on my soul and inner life and be present for my family.

Shabbat is the one day a week when my family will sit down to at least two meals together (Friday night dinner and Shabbat lunch). The children are not rushing to finish their food in order to get to their next activity because the next 'activity' is right there at the table – having a conversation with one another. They know that there are no devices and that no homework, writing or typing can be done on Shabbat. There is nowhere to run to or rush to – it's all happening at home. Shabbat is a Jewish concept (the word and the idea of a sabbatical originated from it) but in our times, some 'unplugged' family time is something we can all adopt every now and then.

My husband and I are blessed with children who have powerful individual souls and strong points of view. They all want a seat at the table. They want to (and should) be listened to at home and at school. As their parents, Yair and I try to influence the direction of our family conversations, because they ultimately shape the culture of the 'company' we're leading – our home, our family. A few years ago, I recognised that too many of our family conversations ended up being negative and critical of each other. Saying we were 'just joking' wasn't a solution, because there was always someone who got emotionally hurt. The children were also comparing and competing with each other (not always, but often enough). I reached a point of frustration and decided to take action. I thought about how I would deal with this in a corporate coaching environment, and I used my consulting skills to create a family game that became known as 'Compliments'.

Friday night became our time for playing 'Compliments'. The game is about introducing the belief that *every family member does good* and it develops the habit of looking for the good in each other, thereby improving everyone's self-esteem. The rule is that during Friday night dinner everyone has to pay at least one compliment to each family member. Every round, one family member is under the 'compliments spotlight', and they receive praise from the rest of us, one after the other. When we first started this, it was a real struggle. My eldest daughter and son couldn't possibly find any compliment to give each other, for weeks! They called each other 'enemies' (needless to say how much that annoyed me) and would argue non-stop at the dinner table. There were times we had long silences as we were waiting to hear compliments and sometimes the big children begged us to skip their turn – they even offered to sacrifice their dessert for a pass! But I made it clear: saying nothing is not an option.

As the weeks and months went by, there was a real shift in our family. We 'discovered' goodness in each other. My son said to his sister, 'I appreciated your help with homework this week when I was stuck with the history assignment,' and his sister said back, 'I know you gave up football training this week so Mum could take me to my dance show. Thank you, I owe you one.' My other son said, 'I saw you helping a child at school during breaktime and I thought that was cool'. And I said to my husband, 'thank you for giving me a hug when I needed it the other day. I know you were crazy busy and left a work call early to see how I was doing.' Yair hugged me again when I complimented him – he knew I'd had a tough week.

After the first few uncomfortable weeks of silence and resistance, giving compliments on Fridays became an enjoyable routine. I knew we were doing something right when my youngest son said to me, 'Mum, I've been spending the whole week looking for things that I can share as a compliment and I can see more of them because I know what I'm looking for.'

Compliments, gratitude and positive feedback are things we can all do more of. For some reason we hold back on saying something good even when complimentary thoughts about others naturally go through our minds. Judaism has a strong focus on showing gratitude. How will our children grow up to be grateful if they don't see us as role models for expressing gratitude?

'I value...', 'I thank...', 'I appreciate...', 'I love...'. By bringing these everyday, yet special words, into the family vocabulary, we can help our children recognise and say good things. Why should we wait for birthdays or big life events like anniversaries or graduations to say all the nice things that are in our hearts? We should say more, today. By making it a family habit to express gratitude and compliment one another, we are not only improving the family experience we have with our children but also teaching them something they will hopefully bring to their future families. And we shouldn't limit ourselves to only giving compliments at home; why not say something kind and meaningful to your colleague, your neighbour or your friends every once in a while?

By the way, it is said that we need to hear ten positive comments for every piece of criticism we are given. Clearly, criticism affects us so much more than praise, which is why we must make ten times the effort to look for the positives in our children.

Give Your Children Vitamin V

Certain aspects of modern culture encourage young people to develop an unhealthy sense of entitlement. It's mostly not their fault; they have just become spoilt by living in a world where things (seem to) come easily. So as soon as they want something, they imagine they deserve it and they become angry, disappointed or frustrated with any parent or authority figure who holds it back from them. Parents often give in, because they don't want to upset their children or because they feel guilty for not giving the child what they ask for. When your children act spoilt or entitled, you must call them out on it. A few weeks ago, my son went to a friend's party and lost his coat there. 'Don't worry *Ima*,' he assured me, 'you can just order another one online. It's on sale now, anyway!' I had to count to ten before I responded – these are the sort of comments that annoy me most. I knew it was a crucial moment to teach him that money is hard-earned and that we don't acquire our possessions through the click of the mouse alone.

So I made him earn the money for the new coat through extra house chores.

It is a parent's job to teach children that what they are needed *for* is often more important than what they need (or think they need), is part of the parent's job, too. The best antidote to entitlement for children (and adults) is a sense of purpose – to know, 'What am I here to do? Who am I here to serve and care for? What is truly meaningful to me?'

One of the ways in which I teach my children to be 'of service' is by volunteering to do charity work as a family – something I think of as 'Vitamin V' (V for volunteering). There is a wonderful organisation in London that supports children and adults with severe learning disabilities. My children know that every week, rain or shine, we are going to spend a few hours offering ourselves as helpers. By now there is little or no resistance because not only do they know that this is not an optional activity, but they also see the value in it and, fortunately, actively enjoy it. The seven years that we have been doing this work have been transformative. It is only through real action, spending time helping others, that a child gradually lets go of the idea that they are owed everything. And it is an activity we can all do together as a family. Introducing volunteering and *tzedakah* into our family has made my children – and myself – understand how fortunate we are and how important it is to serve others, not just ourselves. It is now one of the foundations of our family values. It aims to replace entitlement with purpose.

Acknowledge Your Child's Inner Struggle

My children have a selfish inclination too, just like I do. And just like me, sometimes their natural inclination towards the ego or selfishness wins. They get it wrong. Sometimes they get it very wrong. This is a moment of truth for parents. There are various ways we can respond to 'bad' behaviour. Instead of blaming the child and shaming them, I tell them it's okay to get things wrong. And instead of labelling them with their mistakes, I always remind them that their failures do not define them.

By showing your child that the urge to behave badly or selfishly is something external to their inherently good and pure soul, you can give them a lot of validation. The child is able to stay true to what he or she intuitively knows to be the case – that they are a good person at heart – and they become aware of the constant temptation posed by the bad inclination. They can then learn to combat it. Children feel the internal struggle between their good and bad inclinations, and just like for adults, this tension can scare them, overwhelm them, make them feel weak.

Many children (and adults!) enjoy the idea of admiring, and aspiring to be, heroes. We love watching movies and reading books about our favourite heroes, who often have a strength, quality, personality or mission that we can relate and aspire to. Jewish wisdom uses the word 'hero' in relation to overcoming one's bad inclination:

> Who is considered mighty/a hero? Someone who
> conquers their bad inclination. As it is written, 'Better is

one to slow to anger than a strong man, and one who
rules over his spirit than a conqueror of a city.'
Ethics of the Fathers 4:1

I have found that children relate to this idea – that to be a true hero, they need inner strength more than physical strength. They are inspired to be a hero by developing this internal strength. I find this inspiring too, mainly as a mother. An area in motherhood where my own bad inclination is strong, is controlling my anger. It was never a challenge for me in life before becoming a parent, but for some reason, it's an issue I've struggled with since I became a mother. I work hard on detecting the feeling as it rises inside me; I'm on guard as soon as I start feeling its toxic energy. I aim to be a 'hero' by managing this anger more effectively. I aim to avoid saying something I will later regret, something that I probably don't even mean. And once I control my emotions, when I manage to say what I'm thinking in a much more thoughtful way (or not at all), at that moment, I feel like a 'supermum'!

This approach – recognising and specifically targeting the negative inclinations that challenge us most – sends the message that internal struggle is normal. Everyone, including children – and heroes – is wired with a selfish, negative element that is not going to go away. As long as you are alive, you are going to struggle with its influence – and that's okay. You must reward yourself for your victories and be honest about your failings. But there is no room to be angry about the struggle itself; that's how it is meant to be.

Your child is never bad, and you should never label them as selfish, lazy, unkind or any other negative descriptor. They will sometimes *do* something bad, and you can call them out on that, but try not to do it as a criticism of their actual selves. Let them know they should do things differently next time round, but don't criticise their *essence*. 'That was bad' is so much better than saying, 'You are bad'. It's all too easy for a parent to 'label' their children in their thoughts, reducing them to those one or two things they should improve on: 'they're lazy', 'they're a serial complainer', and so on. But we should try not to; we don't want to define them like that, as if that's their core identity. If we think those things about them, they will sense it and they will identify with these false negative selves.

Turn Your Home into a Small Sanctuary

In Jewish wisdom, the home should be a miniature place of worship; a small sanctuary. Whether you are Jewish or not, if you view your home in this way, you can transform everything that happens there – from eating and drinking to sleeping and studying – into something more meaningful than just the physical activity itself. It can all become part of your shared family culture.

It is your responsibility and opportunity to shape your home into a sanctuary of good values and healthy communication. Your job as a partner and parent is to create a sanctuary, to curate the experiences of your home so that they nourish the heart and the mind. You want your children to feel that their home is a safe, loving, comfortable place and a refuge from the tougher world out there. It should feel like a place where they are accepted and loved for being exactly who they are and a place with clear expectations and boundaries, too. Your home is like a container that 'holds' its family members together in a shared space, in a warm and enabling environment, a place you and they want to be.

This idea perfectly embodies the depth of what a family could become, the meaningful role it can play in your life and your children's lives. Your 'small sanctuary' is not only the physical place where your family lives, but also the safe, comforting environment you have built where your children can feel the ultimate sense of belonging and meaning. The sense of belonging and meaning begins at home. It begins where the child sees the shared values and behaviours of the culture you've created. By participating in those behaviours, the child embraces the culture, which glues them and you together as one unit.

For me, no moment in our week as a family is more of a 'sanctuary' than Shabbat and our Friday night dinners together. The sharing, the bonding, the compliments have shaped us into who we are. All of us look forward to it, even though we sometimes argue. And I try to remember that conflict, when managed well, is healthy and contributes to our growth.

Honour Your Parents

The relationship between children and their parents is deeply important, regardless of how the children feel about the success and effectiveness of their parents' parenting skills. It is no coincidence that one of the most challenging of the Ten Commandments is the commandment to honour one's parents.

> *Honour your father and your mother, that your days may be long.*
> Exodus 20:12

Why does the commandment specifically use the word 'honour' and not another word, like 'love'? Isn't the nature of the parent-child relationship all about love?

Actually, the use of the word 'honour' teaches us a valuable lesson. There may be reasons that children do not love their parents, yet they are still required to honour them. Parents gave their child life. Jewish wisdom teaches that when we dishonour our parents, we dishonour ourselves. The instruction to honour one's parents teaches a child to have gratitude, humility and respect.

I don't know about you, but there have been times when I was furious with my parents, when I was angry and disappointed with them. Those are the times when you want to say the meanest things or do just the opposite – stop communicating, break the relationship. It's okay to have these feelings, they are part of life. But at those times, the expectation to honour my parents helped me. It enabled me not to lose sight of the connection we have purely by the fact that they created me. And if I respect myself and my soul, I must respect them, too. We have a long journey to go on together and these feelings, too, shall pass.

Refine Your Flavour

Your job as a parent is to go with your child on their journey. This doesn't mean you should become their best friend or someone who will do anything they ask. Rather it means we should focus on the key principles that we detailed in this chapter. Assume they have their own way and that you are guiding them on it according to your family values. Let them have a say in what your family values are. Choose to sometimes step aside (*tzimtzum*) to give your child the space they need to grow. By giving them that space when it's needed your influence and guidance will become ever more impactful.

Most important of all: nobody expects you to be a perfect parent – there is no such thing. But it's a good idea to build a vision of how you want to guide and nurture your children, and practise it with love and consistency. The Chassidic leader Rabbi Sholom DovBer Schneersohn once said:

> *It is an unequivocal duty on every individual, from the greatest scholar to the most simple of folk, to set aside a half-hour each day in which to think about the education of their children.*

Make your home a sanctuary built on the three or four values you cherish above all others. Make space for your children's dreams, personalities, emotions, fears and mistakes without overwhelming or controlling them. And in those moments of despair when things are not working, always tell yourself that you are good enough.

If you keep applying yourself, things will work out in the end. Parenting is a long journey, but one that is worth taking.

Educate and Dedicate

When educating our children, we need to teach them according to their way. It is not about what we want them to be, it's about what their souls need them to be. You are there to guide, not control. It is up to you, the parent, to make your home into a safe space for your children, based on higher values. Set boundaries and expectations; let them know the family and humanitarian behaviours you value, but allow them to make their own choices. Create a place where they feel accepted and listened to – and most of all, a place where you can help them discover their individual passions, ambitions and dreams and help guide them on their own journey.

IF YOU CHANGE NOTHING, NOTHING WILL CHANGE

Understanding that we are called to raise our children 'according to their own way' has allowed me to answer questions like: What is my 'role' as a parent? It has also challenged me to think about my role as my parents' child. Looking for the good as a daily practice and sharing compliments at least once a week is a really helpful vehicle for growth and positivity. Reflect on yourself and the people you care about, and answer some or all of these questions in order to see how you could guide your children – or your community, or even yourself – by the soul.

1 How much space do you give your child to grow? To make mistakes? Is it enough?

2 What is the most recent internal or external struggle your child has had? How did you help them through it?

3 List three compliments you would give one of your children or one of your parents.

4 What does your child need from you right now to allow them personal growth? And as someone's child yourself, what do *you* need?

5 What kind of Vitamin V can you start 'taking' at home?

10
RETURN TO YOURSELF

*'Even a little light can dispel
a lot of darkness.'*
The Baal Shem Tov

Five or six years into my learning of Jewish wisdom I realised that I had a purpose, an obligation really: to share the life-changing Jewish principles I had learnt and help others live a meaningful life. I had to share my experience with the many people whose lives could change for the better if only they knew about it, if only they had access to this Jewish wisdom.

Jewish wisdom isn't only for Jews; you know this by now. Its lessons are universal and far reaching. And because people are people no matter what religion they practise, or don't, because all of humanity is struggling with the same difficulties and similar challenges, sharing this wisdom became my mission.

Once I knew that this was my purpose, I revisited my own life experiences and opened up my heart, soul and mind, hoping it would help others. Sharing my personal life didn't come naturally to me. I am a private person, or at least, I used to be, but as Ginni Rometty, IBM CEO once said, 'Growth and comfort do not coexist.' Sharing my story required me to step out of my comfort zone, but I knew that if I wanted to play my part, as someone who cares deeply about people, I'd have to share some of my most private memories, inner feelings and life-changing moments.

I'd like to tell you about one such moment.

When I turned forty-one, I toyed with the idea of trying for a fourth child. Everyone around me either raised their eyebrows or strongly objected. 'Have you lost your mind? Why would you go for a fourth?', 'You're forty-one with three children under ten and you work crazy hours, including international travel. How will you manage?', 'Why would you risk pregnancy at your age?

This could ruin things, Michal. It's a bad idea.' These are just some of the comments I heard.

A few years before this, comments like these would have unsettled me. I would have questioned myself endlessly and assumed the worst possible outcomes, knowing that I would blame myself if anything went wrong. But I have changed so much over the years since I began learning and practising the principles of Jewish wisdom. I was confident enough to believe that the decision was mine and Yair's alone, and I was able to get past the influence and uninvited advice of other people. This was about what we wanted, not what other people thought. And although fear and anxiety weren't totally gone from my system, they were, for the first time in my life, living beside me – not inside me. Fear was no longer all consuming. I became a much stronger, confident and joyful version of myself. And so we decided to go for it, we were keen to parent a new child.

It wasn't just my outlook on life that Jewish wisdom had transformed, but also my most important relationships, including the one with my mother. As a child, I sometimes felt like I'd fallen through the cracks at home. My mother was busy caring for her very sick parents, and after they died within a couple of years of each other, she was consumed by mourning their loss. She truly couldn't see that I was suffering, as a sensitive, frightened young girl. I guess I was wired more for spirituality, while she was wired for survival. I did everything I could to avoid worrying her.

I found myself thinking a lot about my mother during this fourth pregnancy. I learnt that I had been filling myself with the same thoughts and memories of her for too long – and that I was making it all about me. Now that I was a mother myself, and had been 'failing harder' many times throughout the past ten years since becoming a parent, I decided to make space for a new version of our relationship. An opportunity for both of us: a new dialogue, a new creation.

I started working at this and my mother followed along. She learnt to see me the way I wanted her to, and she appreciated my willingness to change as I did hers. Yes, we had difficult conversations as well. Not blaming, 'unfinished business' conversations but compassionate conversations, forgiving conversations, real conversations, where each of us made space for the other's frustration and regret. Both of us emptied ourselves of unhealthy memories and beliefs, and through these meaningful – sometimes painful – conversations, despite and because of our 'brokenness', a new relationship was born.

A few weeks before my baby's due date, I picked up the phone to Tel Aviv, to my mother. 'Mum,' I said, 'I need you by my side in the delivery room. I need *you* holding my hand this time.' It didn't take more than a second for her to reply, 'I'm booking the flight right now.'

During the delivery, I had flashbacks of the times I felt I couldn't 'do' life, the fearful nights, the deep sadness. I remembered all of that, but now there was a healthy separation between my old anxious self and the new version of me. At the miraculous moment of my baby girl's birth, possibly the most elevating experience of my life, I felt like I had given birth to two babies: my baby girl and another newborn – the new version of myself. That's why I *had* to have my mother there with me. So she could be there for my rebirth.

Immediately after my daughter was born, both she and my mother started crying at the same time. My strong, charismatic, beautiful mother's face glowed like never before, and so did mine. I couldn't help thinking that this was our *tikkun*, our repair. What a long way we've travelled to reach this place of love and acceptance. All those years of things unsaid, imaginary expectations and disappointments – they were all part of the journey to reach this moment. The path to get here was long and complex, but it was truly worth it. In fact, there was probably no other way to travel it.

Take the Longer, Shorter Way

Picture the scene: There once was a man who dreamed of visiting the holy Temple in Jerusalem. He had been planning to visit and experience its holiness for his whole life. Finally, the time had arrived to go on the journey. After weeks of travel, he reached a crossroads at the entrance to the city. He didn't know which way to turn. He spotted a young boy sitting there and asked him, 'How can I get to the holy Temple? What is the shortest way?'

The boy pointed and the man set off down that road. But as he got closer to the Temple, the journey became tougher. The path was blocked by bushes and trees. He stumbled and fell, scratched by thorns and branches. The journey became extremely difficult, risky even. The man realised he couldn't reach the Temple this way, so he went back to the crossroads. When the boy saw the man coming back, he seemed unsurprised.

'Why did you send me that way?' asked the man reproachfully. 'Why did you not warn me of all the obstacles?'

'You asked for the shortest way,' said the boy. 'But didn't you know that the shortest way is often the longest way and the longest way is often the shortest? Now, let me show you the longer, shorter way.'

Before I discovered the principles of Jewish wisdom, I was also looking for the shortest possible way to reach my goals. I would become frustrated or disappointed when things didn't go my way. I don't think I was unique in that attitude to life. We live in the age of the internet, and we expect things to happen fast, whether it's our favourite takeaway, online dating or a solution to ageing in the form of lunchtime Botox injections. Even when we try to improve ourselves to become better parents, better leaders, better partners, we often look for the short way: the quick fixes and 'easy' formulas for success. It's difficult to accept that what seems like the shortest way is often the longest, and that it may yield results we didn't bargain for, or no results at all. Sometimes, taking the shortest way means we'll have to start all over again.

At one time or another, if you haven't already, you will find yourself going through a period in which you find your life spiralling downwards, instead of up. When something like this happens to us, it can feel as though we've lost our footing and are sliding downhill, maybe even free-falling. We fear that we will never be able to find our way back, to retrace our steps back up again.

Jewish wisdom tells us:

Every descent is for the sake of the ascent.

This tells us that the descent is *part* of the ascent. It is necessary to go downwards in order to later rise up. Because climbing back up is so difficult, because it's so hard to rise after taking a fall, once we manage to get back on our feet, the ascent is almost inevitable. That the further we fall, the more we work to right ourselves, so the higher we will rise.

It may be that you are trapped by your own self-slavery and are looking for a way to break those internal chains. Or perhaps you are about to rise up from a personal descent and as you rise you want to have a clearer direction of 'travel'. Or maybe you have pivoted from taking the short way, to taking the longer, more meaningful way.

Where are you on your path right now? You probably want to find your way forwards.

Always aim to go forwards, keep on moving, step by step, and even if you slip for a moment, or longer, stand up again and keep climbing. The downward path, narrow bridge or thorny road you are following will lead to a place where you rise stronger, more aware, with more empathy and direction, able to give more and be more than before. It's a long, slow journey at times, but it is the shortest way to a meaningful life.

Finding out not only where you are, but who you were designed to be is the key to building a life without fear. Only when you know your *purpose* can you truly move forward and return to the person you were always meant to be. Let me tell you about the return.

How to Return to Yourself

One of the most fundamental Jewish principles is called *teshuva*. I've already mentioned the holiest day of the Jewish year, Yom Kippur, the Day of Atonement. Yom Kippur is all about the practice of *teshuva*, which is generally understood to mean 'repentance'. Before and during Yom Kippur, we assess our actions over the past year, think about how we can improve, say sorry for any mistakes and make amends.

Traditionally, the idea of 'repentance' has connotations of blame or guilt, but Jewish repentance is much more positive. The literal meaning of *teshuva* is 'return'. It is not a negative process. It is about returning to God, to yourself, to the essence of who you really are, to what you were supposed to be in the first place, to who you were created to become, to your potential. It's about rediscovering your true essence, your eternally good and pure essence, your soul, and focusing on that. It is not about feeling guilt or blaming yourself for your failings. It is about looking at where you are in life, compared to where you have the potential to be, and seeking to course correct.

Returning to yourself can't be done on your own, it requires the participation of others. Apart from a connection to God, which is deeply personal, *teshuva* involves the people you care about as well. And this return is achieved through forgiveness, understanding and tolerance.

Teshuva includes the gift of forgiveness. Not a patronising, passive-aggressive, I-hold-the-power-to-forgive forgiveness, but rather a full-hearted, loving forgiveness that mends and strengthens relationships. One that comes from empathy and love, from accepting that we all fail at times, and from knowing that the descent comes just before the ascent. It takes into account the fact that we learn from our mistakes, that we grow from our brokenness, and that it's these very cracks in our perfection that make us more beautiful, more complete.

Asking for forgiveness is therefore an expectation, a condition of our *teshuva*. We might hurt people on the longer, shorter way, by mistake and sometimes on purpose. There is no way we can evolve and proceed on the journey if we leave loose ends and unresolved conflict behind. Forgiving and asking for forgiveness are both powerful ways to cross your bridges. Forgiving replaces fear and anger with compassion and kindness. It recharges us.

Jewish wisdom tells us that when we sleep, our souls ascend to heaven to recharge. Every time you wake up, it's a renewed vote of confidence, a sign. A sign that G-d chose to return your soul to your body and grant you once again the gift of life. Every single moment you breathe is a reminder that you are here for a reason, that there is a task for you to fulfil.

It's so easy to forget this meaningful opportunity. Every day is an opportunity for growth, every moment has potential for change. Every morning, I say the Jewish morning prayer. The moment I open my eyes, I say it out loud, before any other words come out of my mouth. I use this as a daily reminder to be grateful for life itself and what we can make of it, each and every day.

This is the short yet powerful morning prayer, known as *Modeh Ani*:

מודה אני לפניך מלך חי וקיים שהחזרת
בי נשמתי בחמלה. רבה אמונתך

I offer thanks to You, living and eternal King,
for You have mercifully restored my soul
within me; Your faithfulness is great.
Siddur

This prayer is a source of inspiration for me, because if God believes in me, in the soul within me, then I should certainly believe in myself.

Each day when you wake up, it is a spiritual wake-up, too. Your soul has been restored once more. In the same way, *teshuva* is not a one-off act. It isn't something you do once in a lifetime, or even once a year. You can do a little bit of *teshuva* every single day, and focus on how you treat others and yourself, remembering what you are here to be and to do. It's true for people, it's true for companies, it's true for families, it's true for parents and their children and it's true for you.

We can all do a little *teshuva* – today. Right now. You have the power to assess where you are and where you ought to be. View every single day as an opportunity to adjust, to correct, to forgive or be forgiven, to reflect and evaluate and to always, *always*, move forward.

The greatest lesson I learnt from Jewish wisdom is that life is not a challenge to be overcome, to be solved. It's an experience to be lived. I am not a problem to be fixed.

Neither are you. You are a complex, beautiful human being designed to grow, improve and become who you were always supposed to be. None of us are here by chance, we are all here for a reason. The world needs us to do something, finding that purpose is one of our life missions.

The Jewish wisdom in this book is about moving onwards and upwards, about finding that constantly flickering, upwards-reaching, beautiful flame inside us. It's about looking at life not as a puzzle to be solved but as a series of bridges to cross. It's about seizing the chance to be the unique person you were designed to be in the first place.

The journey is happening right now. There is so much ahead of you: tall bridges and narrow paths to cross, never ending potential and endless opportunities for *tikkun* and *teshuva*. You and I are on a life-changing journey – we all are. It won't be short and easy, and neither should it be, but it is the only way to find inner peace, purpose and joy.

Ask yourself:

What would you do if you weren't afraid?

Return and Repent

The Hebrew word for 'repentance', **teshuva**, actually means 'return'. This reflects the idea that to repent we should return to our true, essentially good essence. It shows us a way to improve ourselves and overcome the obstacles we face without feeling guilt or shame. Instead of blaming ourselves for our shortcomings, we should assess where we are on our path, compared to where we should be – where our soul wants us to be – and course correct. If we regularly think about how to return to our essence and our own unique path, we will be able to always move forward with purpose, with meaning and without fear.

IF YOU CHANGE NOTHING, NOTHING WILL CHANGE

Grab a cup of tea, coffee or water and a pen, and make space to reflect on these questions. Remember – this is for your own personal learning, no one is reading or watching you, and there are no right or wrong answers. Your soul is unique. Only you know the flame inside you, only you can access your soul. But while this is your unique journey, you are not alone, and we can seek the way forward together. At the end of this book, just a few pages away, is a glossary, which includes many of the Jewish terms and principles I have shared with you. As you answer the following questions, I invite you to revisit the ideas that could change your outlook on life. Be open-minded and open-hearted. Be true to yourself. Be curious. By now we know that if you change nothing, nothing will change. Even one little step forward will make a big difference.

1 Consider how you felt when you picked up this book. What did you hope to find?

2 Where are you today, right now, on your journey? What 'bridge' are you are planning to cross soon?

3 What is your way across that bridge? What actions or mindshift do you need to take?

4 What is your soul telling you about what it's here to do? What are your thoughts on your purpose right now? What great things you are here to be and do?

5 What in your life can you repair? What needs *tikkun*?

6 What do you think is your narrow straits, those thoughts or beliefs that might hold you back from crossing that bridge?

7 Think about *tzimtzum*. What and who do you need to make more space for?

8 How far away are you from the person you are designed to be? How could you make a start at returning?

9 Your brokenness is your completeness. Remind yourself what is wonderful about the *whole* you. What makes the space between the pieces of your heart so special?

10 What is first step you will take to move forward on your journey?

Glossary

Ayeka

A Hebrew word that means 'Where are you?' This is the first question asked in the Torah, by God to Adam, after Adam and Eve sinned in the Garden of Eden. God asked Adam, 'Where are you?' not because He did not know where Adam was physically. The question was an invitation – a wake-up call – asking where Adam was spiritually and existentially.

Chassidism

A movement founded by the Baal Shem Tov in eighteenth-century eastern Europe with the aim of revealing the soul in every person and every experience, thereby bringing joy and meaning to the everyday practice of Judaism. The Baal Shem Tov revitalised the Jewish communities who were struggling to connect with God in their day-to-day life. Many eastern European Jews at that time did not have a deep understanding of the Torah, or even access to Torah learning. Chassidism sought to make spirituality accessible and part of everyday life. There are various branches of Chassidism, some of which, such as

Chabad, take an intellectual approach to spirituality, while others, such as Breslov, focus on an emotional connection with God.

Chassidut
The teachings of Chassidism. Beginning with the Baal Shem Tov, Chassidic leaders produced a body of literature that expresses the philosophy and teachings of Chassidism.

chuppah
A Jewish wedding canopy, under which the bride and groom stand during the marriage ceremony. It is traditionally comprised of a cloth, supported by four poles. It symbolises the divine protection that encompasses the newlyweds and the home that the new couple will build for themselves.

Holocaust
The genocide of six million European Jews, including 1.5 million children, by the Nazis during the Second World War. Initially, Jewish people across Europe were segregated in ghettos and detention centres, their businesses boycotted and their human rights ignored. In 1942, Adolf Hitler's Final Solution – his policy to exterminate Jews – was put into practice. Jews were rounded up by the Nazis and their collaborators. Some were murdered immediately, while others were sent on trains to concentration camps and death camps, where many were murdered in gas chambers. Families were torn apart, some never to see each other again. Conditions in the ghettos and camps were horrific; inmates were

subjected to squalor, starvation, disease, forced labour and cruel medical experiments. Approximately two thirds of the Jewish population of Europe was decimated.

Kabbalah

A discipline of Jewish mysticism that explores the purpose of creation and the mysteries of the cosmos and the soul. The foundational Kabbalistic text, the *Zohar*, was composed in the second century by Rabbi Shimeon Bar Yochai and published in the thirteenth century. The teachings of Kabbalah, based on the *Zohar* and other mystical works, developed over the generations, until they were defined and codified by Rabbi Isaac Luria, a sixteenth-century mystic in the town of Safed, Israel. The Kabbalah is often regarded as the 'Soul of the Torah', through which one can discover the inner meaning of its words, as well as the Torah secrets on how to live meaningfully. *Chassidut* is the modern-day application of Kabbalah, meant to inspire and help the individual self-improve by becoming more aware of and connected to their soul and true essence – to bring holiness into everyday life.

kelipa

The Hebrew word for 'shell' or 'bark'. In Kabbalah, *kelipa* refers to a metaphysical barrier, or shell, that conceals the divine (soul) from the physical world. Essentially, *kelipa* refers to anything that is not aware of the divine 'spark' within.

mensch

The Yiddish word for 'a good person' – someone of integrity and honour. A *mensch* is known particularly for choosing to do the right thing for the benefit of others, and for following their good inclination more often than their bad inclination. 'Being a *mensch*' is considered a great compliment.

Modeh Ani

The morning prayer that is meant to be the first words uttered by a Jewish person when they wake up in the morning. *Modeh Ani* means 'I give thanks'. The prayer is an act of gratitude to God for choosing to return one's soul to their body after sleep, and to once again grant them the gift of life. It's a daily reminder that every day is a new beginning and a new opportunity for growth and meaning.

Passover

A Jewish festival celebrated in the spring to commemorate how God freed the Israelites from hundreds of years of slavery in Egypt. Passover is celebrated for eight days (seven in Israel), during which Jews are forbidden to eat leavened foods (foods that have risen, for example bread). The first two nights of Passover (only one in Israel) are celebrated with a ritual meal, known as the Seder, during which families gather to recall and discuss the exodus from Egypt. Passover has a deep spiritual meaning that focuses on humility, self-awareness and transcendence.

Rebbe

A Yiddish variation of the word 'Rabbi'. Both 'Rabbi' and 'Rebbe' come from the Hebrew word *rav*, which means 'master', 'teacher' or 'mentor'. 'Rebbe' is now commonly used to indicate a righteous and spiritual leader of a Chassidic movement.

Yom Kippur

The holiest day of the Jewish calendar. Yom Kippur is the Day of Atonement, a twenty-five-hour fast, when Jewish people pray to God for a happy, healthy year ahead. On Yom Kippur (and in the weeks leading up to it) Jewish people do *teshuva*. They reflect on their mistakes and failures, apologise to those they've wronged, and to God, and plan for how they will move forward and grow, becoming a better version of themselves.

Shabbat

The Jewish day of rest, which begins at sundown every Friday and lasts until nightfall on Saturday. The Hebrew root of the word 'Shabbat' means 'to rest'. During Shabbat, Jewish people are forbidden to do any work. The definition of 'work' includes cooking, driving, writing and the use of electrical items, among many other things. Traditionally, on Friday night, Shabbat is welcomed in (eighteen minutes before sundown) with the lighting of the Shabbat candles and a special blessing. Shabbat is a holy day that involves spiritual focus – prayer, festive family meals and connection to the wider community. It's a unique time to reflect on the week that has passed and connect to one's soul.

tikkun olam

A Hebrew phrase that means 'repairing the world'. In Judaism, *tikkun olam* refers to a person's responsibility for the welfare of their community, society, and the world as a whole. As a concept, *tikkun olam* has become fairly well-known universally as a call for social and environmental justice.

yetzer hara

The inclination to do bad things. It is one of the two core desires of every person (opposing the good inclination, the *yetzer tov*), but it does not define a person's true essence. We battle the *yetzer hara*, which tempts us to follow our selfish impulses. Overcoming this urge on a daily basis is what makes us human and is a sign of personal development and growth. It is not to be destroyed, but rather tamed or conquered.

yetzer tov

The inclination to do good things. It is one of the two core desires of every person (opposing the bad inclination, the *yetzer hara*). The tension between these two inclinations and our ability to choose one over the other is how we grow. The struggle of our own internal forces is the ultimate vehicle for self-improvement.

Jewish Texts

Ecclesiastes
A Biblical book of wisdom. According to rabbinic tradition, it was written by King Solomon.

Ethics of the Fathers
A tractate of the Mishna that focuses on moral and ethical matters.

Etz Chaim
The foundational text of modern (Lurianic) Kabbalah. It contains the teachings of Rabbi Isaac Luria, as recorded by his disciple, Rabbi Chaim Vital. First published in 1573, *Etz Chaim* details Luria's system of Kabbalah, from the divine order and God's creation of the world to our perception of reality.

Mishna
A collection of six orders, each one containing a number of tractates, that record the oral laws and traditions of Judaism. The Mishna was compiled in the third century by Rabbi Judah ha-Nasi. It makes up part of the Talmud.

Proverbs
A Biblical book of wisdom. According to rabbinic tradition, it was written by King Solomon.

Siddur
The Jewish prayer book that contains the daily prayers, weekly Shabbat prayers and holidays prayers, as well as prayers recited at various occasions.

Song of Songs
A Biblical allegorical love poem. According to rabbinic tradition, it was written by King Solomon.

Talmud
The central text of Jewish religious law that was compiled in the fifth century. It contains the oral teachings of the Jewish sages (the Mishna) and their discussions of the legal, ethical, spiritual, intellectual and historical aspects of Jewish law. These rabbinic discussions on the Mishna are knows as the Gemara. There are six volumes of the Talmud, within which are sixty-three tractates, each expounding on a different subject.

Tanya
The *Tanya* is the foundational text of Chabad *Chassidut*, a branch of Chassidism that takes an intellectual approach to spirituality. Written by Rabbi Shneur Zalman of Liadi and published in 1796, the *Tanya* offers guidance and advice – based on Kabbalah (Jewish mysticism) and earlier teachings – to help people in their practical service of God and personal spiritual growth.

Torah

The word 'Torah' means 'teachings' or 'guidance'. The Torah is the foundational text of Judaism. It is the holiest of all books – a blueprint and guide to living a Jewish life. The Torah is the written texts of Judaism, comprised of five books: *Genesis*, *Exodus*, *Leviticus*, *Numbers* and *Deuteronomy* (although the term 'Torah' is often used to refer to Jewish teachings in general). The Torah includes the narrative of history and Judaism: from the creation of the universe and the human race, the lives of the Patriarchs and Matriarchs, the slavery in and exodus from Egypt, how the Jewish people became a holy nation, through to the Jewish people receiving the Ten Commandments at Sinai and wandering for forty years in the desert before arriving at the land of Israel. The Torah also includes the laws of Judaism, as relayed by Moses from God to the people. According to Judaism, the Torah was transcribed by Moses from God's words. Often, people use the term Torah to mean Hebrew Bible, although technically, the complete Hebrew Bible is called the Tanach, which contains the Torah as well as two other collections of Jewish texts: Prophets and Chronicles – a total of twenty-four books. The Torah, however, is revered most highly of these texts because it is defined as the word of God.

Zohar

The foundational work of Kabbalah, Jewish mysticism. The *Zohar* was composed by Rabbi Shimeon Bar Yochai in the second century and published in the thirteenth century by Rabbi Moses de Leon. The *Zohar* contains esoteric commentary on the Torah and mystical discussions about God, the creation of the universe and the nature of souls.

Bibliography

Angel, Marc (ed.), *The Koren Pirkei Avot (Ethics of the Fathers)*, Hebrew and English edition, Koren Publishers, Jerusalem, 2015.

Artscroll (ed.), *Mishnah Bava Basra/Sanhedrin*, The Ryzman Edition, Mesorah Publications, Ltd., Brooklyn, 2016.

Brown, Brené at the Society for Human Resource Management Annual Conference & Exposition, Las Vegas, 2019.

Brown, Brené, *Dare to Lead: Brave Work. Tough Conversations. Whole Hearts.*, Random House, New York, 2018.

Buckingham, Marcus and Donald O. Clifton, *Now, Discover your Strengths*, The Free Press, New York, 2001.

Frank, Anne, *Anne Frank: The Diary of a Young Girl*, Doubleday, New York, 1952.

Frankl, Viktor E., *Man's Search for Meaning*, gift edition, Beacon Press, Boston, 2014 (first published in 1946).

Frankl, Viktor E., *The Unheard Cry for Meaning: Psychotherapy and Humanism*, Simon & Schuster, New York, 2011.

Frankl, Viktor E., *The Will to Meaning*, New American Library, New York, 1988.

Freud, Sigmund, 'Recommendations to Physicians Practising Psycho-analysis', 1912.

Freud, Sigmund, *Moses and Monotheism*, Alfred A. Knopf, New York, 1939.

Grant, Adam, 'Stop Trying to Raise Successful Kids', *The Atlantic*, 2019.

Grant, Adam, *Give and Take: A Revolutionary Approach to Success*, Wiedenfield & Nicholson, London, 2013.

Jacobson, Simon, *60 Days: A Spiritual Guide to the High Holidays*, Meaningful Life Center, 2018.

Lencioni, Patrick, *The Five Dysfunctions of a Team*, Jossey-Bass, San Fracisco, 2002.

Matt, Daniel C. (translator), *Zohar*, The Pritzker Edition, Stanford University Press, Palo Alto, 2003 (first published in the thirteenth century).

Patterson, Kerry, Joseph Grenny, Ron McMillan and Al Switzler, *Crucial Conversations: Tools for talking when stakes are high*, McGraw-Hill, New York, 2002.

Scherman, Rabbi Nosson and Meir Zlotowitz, (eds.), *The Complete Artscroll Siddur*, Mesorah Publications, Ltd., Brooklyn, 1984.

Scherman, Rabbi Nosson (ed.), *Tanach*, The Stone Edition, Mesorah Publications, Ltd., Brooklyn, 1996.

Taylor, Bill, 'Write a Failure Résumé to Learn What Makes You Succeed', *Harvard Business Review*, 2016.

Vital, Rabbi Chaim, *Etz Chaim*, Barazani, 2004.

Winnicott, Donald W., *Playing and Reality*, Tavistock, London, 1971.

Zalman, Rabbi Shneur, *Tanya*, Kehot Publication Society, Brooklyn, 2014 (first published 1796).

Index

Acknowledgments

It takes a village to write a book, or at least it did in my case. There's no way I could have written and published *What Would You Do If You Weren't Afraid?* without my amazing community of supporters, guides, critics and mentors.

Thank you to:

Dr Naftali Loewenthal, for planting the idea of writing a book in my mind and supporting me with your advice.

Rabbi Gordon, for teaching me the wisdom of *Chassidut* and for inspiring thousands of students on their journeys towards living meaningfully.

Dr Asi Sharabi, for being such a brilliant visionary, connector and creative. For being the brilliant matchmaker between agent, publisher and me. Your faith in me, and the book, gave me confidence.

Yanetz Levi, for being my loving brother-in-law, confidant and advisor. You always listen with care and patience. Your advice got me out of scary self-doubt moments and your feedback made everything better.

Rebecca Smart, for being a leader who makes space for diverse voices. For being bold and honest, generously opening doors with endless opportunities. For being my mentor.

Stephanie Milner, for being a trusted partner, for co-piloting the mission with much passion and drive, and for being open and curious.

Marleigh Price, for your guidance and collaboration, in creating this beautiful paperback together.

The Blair Partnership team: Rory Scarfe, for spotting the book's potential from the very beginning and immediately believing in and supporting the book – and for believing in me, too – and Neil Blair, for all of your advice, guidance and faith in the cause.

Sophie Bradshaw, for holding my hand on those wobbly first steps, for our deep brainstorm sessions and for leading us forward when I was stuck and overwhelmed.

Orna Landau, for taking us to the finish line, saying what needed to be said and keeping it real. For caring from deep inside and working to crazy deadlines.

Shari Last, for your deep care, professionalism and great attention to the details that matter. For always going the extra mile, researching and improving to perfection.

Rabbi Jacobson, for your wisdom, guidance and encouragement. For your inspirational books and writings that were among the first things I read on my learning path.

Bess Daly, Christine Keilty, Nicola Powling and Luke Bird, for always being open minded, pushing the boundaries of creativity and making the book look as good as it does. And for making it a fun creative experience all along!

Tom Leighton, for capturing the position that represents 'me' on camera – and a photoshoot day to remember.

Galia Verthime Sherf, for taking the picture that became my author profile image. You understood intuitively what I was looking for.

Anna Paynton and Gayley Avery, for your brilliant PR and marketing knowledge, your excitement and drive, and for your team's dedication around the globe.

Maud Watson and Elise Italiaander, for helping me find my voice on audio and for giving me the confidence to record my journey and my learnings.

Marc Maley, for being the brilliant brand strategist you are, for teaching me things I didn't know. For your passion, endless optimism and the sparkle in your eye.

Chani Lieberman, for always being there with much care and good advice. For your deep knowledge and understanding of *Chassidut*. For guiding me and knowing what I needed to learn and when.

Batsheva Lazar, for holding my hand during ascents and descents on the learning journey. For answering my hard questions with a loving heart and a kind soul.

Facebook, the company, for being my 'workplace home' for many years. For being a place that gave me space to grow myself, and to help others grow.

Lady Nicola Mendelsohn, for being my inspiration. For your passion for living a meaningful life. Your mentorship and encouragement meant the world to me.

Igal Padida, for your creativity, honesty, patience and big heart. For your art that heals hearts.

Dr Baruch Kahana, for your deep listening, sensitivity and encouragement. For making 'space'.

Yonat Meirson, Shiri Amsalem, Mickey Slonim and

Tal Shuster, for being my life friends since our army days together, and for always being there for me. For the 'real conversations' we had about this book and our journey and for how we believe in and empower each other.

Kat Gray, for being my brilliant, supportive manager at Facebook and for giving me confidence and help along the way. You role model the leadership qualities I find most inspiring.

Jonny Geller, for your honesty and your belief that the world needs to know this wisdom.

TikTok, the company, for welcoming me with much love and care, and for wanting to do great things together.

Boba and Tuti, for your endless love and deep commitment to our family. You are part of our family and without you I wouldn't have been able to birth this book baby, too.

And now to the beautiful souls that I am proud to call my family:

My loving parents, Masha and Jehuda Hiss, for giving me life. For always being there, for evolving as parents and humans, and choosing to learn and see new wonders. I am proud to be your daughter. Thank you for teaching me family values, resilience and respect.

My sister, Dana Amirav, for your honesty, passion and curiosity, for loving from all your heart. For arriving in our family when we were missing exactly you.

My wonderful Oshmans:

Yair, every day I thank God for hooking us up together. There is no one in this world who understands me better than you do. Your love, care and faith in our family makes us all stronger. You give us the confidence to believe that there is nothing we can't achieve in life. Your endless positivity and energy are our family's fuel. Thank you for choosing me for the 'longer, shorter way' of life and for helping me believe in myself.

Our children, you are our greatest pride and joy. We love you endlessly. Thank you:

Tamar, for making me a mother and trusting me along the way. For being the kindest soul and for your deep belief in people's goodness and potential. For being humble and value driven. Your smile melts my heart every time I see you.

Yoav, for maximising every opportunity life presents you and always thinking big, deep and meaningful. For your sensitive soul and your big heart. For seeing beyond what many of us can see, searching for the truth and essence of life itself. For always trying harder, with great passion. You are the greatest forgiver I know.

Ari, for being our family's 'sunshine', bringing light, joy and positivity to our home and hearts. For being passionate about practising our faith and teaching us new things every Shabbat. We always feel at home in your presence

Eliya, for being our family's cherry on top; you completed us from the moment you arrived in the world. For being a real wonder – sharing with us your love for life. You bring joy in ways that are truly magical. We are all crazy in love with you.

For grandmother Chana, who is my inspiration. Thank you for taking *that* jump!

For the Hiss, Kanner and Arbitman family members

who survived the trauma of the Holocaust and still carried on with life, moving forward and upwards, never giving up on hope. I felt your hurting hearts and souls, and your essence lives within us, always.

For those who did not survive the war, this is for you, too. You are a living memory within us and within our eternal nation's story.

About the Author

Behind the façade of a picture-perfect life, Michal Oshman grappled with the inherited trauma of her Holocaust-surviving grandparents. Bearing the scars of a family torn apart by war, Michal also found herself exposed to crime and violence through her father's role as a chief forensic pathologist and coroner. Overwhelmed by fear and anxiety, she searched for solace and healing, only to find herself trapped in a maze of conventional psychotherapy.

Until, at last, she unearthed a long-hidden wisdom, a secret formula that had survived the ages, waiting to be discovered. This ancient knowledge transformed her life, shattering the chains of fear and anxiety that had held her captive for so long. It redefined her career, invigorated her relationships, and reshaped her approach to parenting. Now, Michal Oshman has made it her life's purpose to share her journey and the secret formula that changed her life, empowering others to break free from the grasp of fear and embrace their fullest potential.

A seasoned leader in the Technology and Entertainment industries, Michal has worn many hats over her illustrious career. Formerly the Head of Company Culture at TikTok and International Leadership Development Executive at Facebook (Meta), Michal has guided and mentored hundreds of business leaders across the globe. Holding three university degrees in psychology and sociology, she is also a veteran military officer, a TEDx speaker, and an international bestselling author. Michal lives in London, UK, with her husband and their four children. You can find out more information about Michal at www.michaloshman.com

DK LONDON
Senior Acquisitions Editor
Stephanie Milner
Development Editors
Marleigh Price, Orna Landau
Jacket Co-ordinator Jasmin Lennie
Pre-production Manager
Sunil Sharma
DTP Designers Manish Chandra
Uperti, Umesh Rawat
Production Editor David Almond
Senior Production Controller
Stephanie McConnell
Art Director Maxine Pedliham
Publishing Director Katie Cowan

Copy Editor Shari Last
Proofreader and Indexer
Elizabeth Dowsett
Jacket Designer
The Book Designers

This edition publishied
in Great Britain in 2023
First published in Great Britain in
2021 by Dorling Kindersley Limited
DK, One Embassy Gardens,
8 Viaduct Gardens,
London, SW11 7BW

Copyright © 2021, 2023
Dorling Kindersley Limited
A Penguin Random House Company
10 9 8 7 6 5 4 3 2
003–336277–May/2023

Text copyright © 2021,
2023 Michal Oshman
Michal Oshman has asserted her
right to be identified as
the author of this work
Cover photograph by
Galia Verthime Sherf

The phrase 'What Would You Do If
You Weren't Afraid?' first appears in
Who Moved My Cheese? by Dr
Spencer Johnson, published by G.P.
Putnam's Sons in 1998.

A CIP catalogue record for this book
is available from the British Library.
ISBN: 978-0-2416-2815-7

Printed and bound in
the United Kingdom

www.dk.com

This book is a work of non-fiction
based on the life, experiences and
recollections of Michal Oshman. In
some cases, names of people and
places have been changed solely to
protect the privacy of others.

MIX
Paper | Supporting
responsible forestry
FSC™ C018179

This book was made with Forest
Stewardship Council™ certified
paper – one small step in DK's
commitment to a sustainable future.
**For more information go to
www.dk.com/our-green-pledge**